BE: THE WAY OF REST

A Holistic Recipe for Walking with Jesus

Jim Stern

Published by Trexo
Houston, Texas

Be: The Way of Rest
A Holistic Recipe for Walking with Jesus

© 2015 by Jim Stern

Published in Houston, Texas by Trexo.

Edited by Blake Atwood with EditFor.me.

CONTENTS

ACKNOWLEDGMENTS

This book took sixteen years to write. For the first thirteen, I was discipled and discipled others. For the last three, I've led a disciple-making movement, one person at a time, called CORE in Houston, Texas.

Jesus saved me when I was twenty-six. Soon thereafter He introduced me to two men, David Glenn and Mark Collins. They discipled me. For no reason other than the love of Jesus, these men opened their hearts and homes to me and trained me how to walk with the Lord. Being new to the faith, I thought this was normal. Much later, I found out it wasn't.

Nevertheless, their discipling set me on a path of personal discipleship that carried into my ministry within the churches I've served and ultimately formed CORE's foundation. In January 2013, I founded Trexo, a ministry that equips disciples to make disciples. Through Trexo we have opportunities to help people, churches, and other organizations develop effective disciple-making methods and strategies. In brief, CORE is people, Trexo is resources.

I would like to thank:

My Father in Heaven, Jesus, and the Holy Spirit for calling me out of darkness and showering me with love, restoration, and life. I am still stunned that I can enter the throne of grace with confidence. Father, I am overwhelmed by the wisdom you give and the perfection of Your ways. You are the Answer.

Jesus, the life I feel when I speak your name is intoxicating. You bring me to tears and fill me with inexpressible joy. This book is about Your life and how You have taught me to walk in it.

Holy Spirit, you are mysteriously fantastic. You are teaching me to hear and discern. You show me landmines before me. You give me words to speak to my wife, to my children, and to others. I am awe-filled in simple reflection that I am a child of the one true God who reigns and rules over all His creation.

To Brett Russell: God used you in those fourteen-hour days at Aerotek to open my eyes to Him. You were a powerful weapon in my life.

To David Glenn and Mark Collins, the men who first discipled me: I would not be who I am—disciple, husband, father, pastor—without either one of you, no matter how much you both want to play down your influence in my life! This book would not exist without your investment in me.

To my wife, Brooke, who is my flesh and my bones: you have more belief in Jesus' work in me than I do, and your support has carried me when I have needed to be carried. I could not do this or be who I am without you. Together we have known so much of our Father's faithfulness. I love you deeply.

ACKNOWLEDGMENTS

To Collin and Claire, my kiddos: (We named Collin after Mark Collins.) At the time of this writing they are seven and five, respectively. They daily challenge me to simplify my teaching. They help me understand the love of the Father.

To my mother, Peggy, and my father, Scott, for your support and belief.

To Ben Butler, Director of the Way of the Cross: Wow! Through you I saw living miracles. Thank you for teaching me about missions and trusting God to do the craziest, most unthinkable things every day.

To John Bisagno, Pastor Emeritus of Houston's First Baptist Church: why you would spend time with someone like me is beyond me. Thank you for teaching me how to love people and for loving me.

To Luis Valdes, Mike Sellars (and of course Schon), Tim McInturf and Greg Dugi, my brothers with whom I have walked through hell and back: we have come so far and yet have so far to go. (I rotate through these men so as not to burn any one of them out!)

To all of those who have allowed me to invest in your life, thank you for your openness to the Lord and to me. In particular, thank you, Chris Garcia, for following the call of God on your life, walking away from other, more stable opportunities and joining me in in all of this! God has great things.

To my CORE family: thank you for allowing me to experiment on you, for allowing the Holy Spirit to open your hearts, and for believing that Jesus will absolutely teach you to be fishers of men.

I have learned through writing this book that a major difference exists between good speaking and good writing. I am indebted to my brother David Stern, Alice Haagen, Bonnie Walker, Matt Trozzo, Mark Collins, Luis Valdes, and Waters Davis for their editing work. If the language of this book is smooth and flows well, it is because these people hammered and chiseled the rock I gave them!

I am a very blessed man by the quantity and quality of people in my life that I truly love and who truly love me. Thank you for allowing me to have a part in your relationship with our Father.

Now let us go, in the power of the Holy Spirit according to the will of our Father, and make disciples of Jesus!

BE

THE WAY OF REST

FOREWORD: A BRIEF STORY

In early 2010, I was in a dark place. I sought help from Tom Billings, the director of the Union Baptist Association in Houston. He was exceedingly busy, but made time for me and graciously listened to my story. When I finished, he gave me an assignment.

He told me that somehow Jesus had lived His life as a "non-anxious" presence. I was to study the Gospels and figure out what Jesus knew and how He had lived that allowed Him to live in that way. Six chapters into the book of Mark, *The Way of Rest* took shape.

About that same time I had lunch with David Glenn and Mark Collins, the men who first discipled me. I shared my story with them as well. David, who had just returned to the States from a work assignment in Australia, said to me, "Mate, you need rest. Jesus said, 'Come to Me all who are weary and heavy laden and I will give you rest.'"

My Father used my dark place and those two conversations to begin a journey into discovering Jesus' way of rest that would take me three years to write—and a lifetime to walk.

BE

THE WAY OF REST

INTRODUCTION: WHAT IS BGM?

Christianity has two great needs today: the development of simple, holistic methods of walking with Jesus and for veteran Christians who bear the marks of life in the Kingdom to go and invest in the lives of others, discipling them to maturity.

Why do we need a holistic method of walking with Jesus? Jesus declared that He is "the way, the truth, and the life" (John 14:16). He lived His life in a certain way and according to certain truths that produced life. We have many books written on the truth of Jesus laid out in an orderly way. However, we have very few books that lay out an order of the way of Jesus. We have even fewer books that help us connect Jesus' way according to Jesus' truth that produce Jesus' life.

Where is the life in His people? So many brothers and sisters are confused in their faith. What pieces of the faith they have are disconnected from each other. Significant aspects of walking with Jesus are missing. Consequently, many followers of Jesus live difficult lives knowing there is something more, but are unable to talk about it, and they tend to believe that there's nowhere to find answers.

We need direction and structure. We need methods of walking with Jesus that give us clarity in how we can live the life He came to give us.

Why do we need disciples to make disciples (who make more disciples)? Simply put, because Jesus made disciples, His followers made disciples, and He commands all Christians to go and do the same (Matthew 28:18–20). He does not command *the church* to make disciples, He commands *believers*. Christianity is most powerful when followers of Jesus, equipped with simple methods, spread the Gospel one person at a time. The work of the Holy Spirit to change people is an underground, grassroots, "of the people," disciple-making movement.

As a follower of Jesus, Paul writes in Philippians 3:17, "Brethren, join in following my example, and observe those who walk according to the pattern you have in us." Paul walks with Jesus according to a certain pattern. He has trained a generation of believers in Philippi to walk in his pattern. Now he is exhorting a new generation to follow his example and observe those he has already trained. Paul is a veteran disciple making disciples according to a relational methodology, who then become examples themselves to a new generation!

Holding to Jesus' standard that we are not training for the sake of training, but so that people can experience life, does Paul's method pass the test? Paul writes in Philippians 4:9, "The things you have learned and received and heard and seen in me, practice these things, and the God of peace will be with you." He confidently knows that his way of walking with Jesus *will* produce the peace of God in a person. His way is not a theory. It is not abstract. Paul's way of life works. His way passes the test.

Whatever our pattern of walking with Jesus is, our standard must be the life Jesus came to offer.

WHAT IS BGM?

BGM is our discipleship ministry's method for walking with Jesus and a strategy for reproducing disciples.

Through BGM, any person will be trained to:

- **BE** a disciple.
- **GO** share with others.
- **MAKE** those who accept Jesus' invitation into disciples.

BGM starts with being.

Jesus is the Son of His Father. He lived in intimacy with the Holy Spirit. His identity was secure. He knew who He was and whose He was. That foundation anchored Him and sustained Him in the war of life. Clarifying *being* is the essential core of life in Jesus' way.

In fact, I argue that the reason many people do not *go and make* is because they are confused, compartmentalized, or compromised in *being*. Their unhealthy being produces lives that are not enviable. They know it. Therefore, they do not want to go and make.

BE   GO   MAKE

Figure 1: A diagram of BGM methodology.

They do not believe anyone would want what they have. Through being we seek to clarify issues of identity, releasing the power and love of the reality that we, like Jesus, are sons and daughters of the Father and temples of the Holy Spirit.

From being, BGM moves to going.

Going is faithfully following the Holy Spirit's direction to share the Gospel of the Kingdom. Jesus commissions all of us in Matthew 28:19, "Go and make disciples." How do we succeed in this? We need to know whom we are to share with and what we are to share. We need effective tools. In going, we examine Jesus' methods and the methods of the disciples to glean what they have for us today. As the Spirit equips us as we go!

Finally, in BGM we are equipped to make.

Making is being faithful to the Spirit to shepherd a person from an unbeliever to one who is maturing in the faith and will reproduce the Kingdom in others. We look at effective strategies and structures for making disciples. As we go to make, we are training people to be. Our making becomes their being. And the process repeats itself as the Spirit leads faithful men and women in the mess of making disciples who make disciples.

BGM is an effective, holistic strategy to be followers of Jesus who are faithfully going, equipped to make reproducing disciples. BGM is taught through a three-book series: *BE: The Way of Rest* and the forthcoming titles *Go* and *Make*.

In addition to these titles, Trexo also has *The On Ramp* and *FORTIFIED*. *The On Ramp* is nine introductory sessions for someone who is new or newer to the Lord. In *The On Ramp*, a person will be trained to effectively use the Lord's Prayer as Jesus intended. Videos for each session and free downloads are available at Trexo.org.

FORTIFIED is a method for helping people find freedom in Jesus. The Holy Spirit continually leads us to people who are suffering various forms of bondage. *FORTIFIED* is the method we use to identify and overcome areas of darkness.

All of these resources are available through Trexo.org and are designed to equip disciples to be, go, and make disciples.

1: ASLEEP IN THE STORM

Jesus had spent the day teaching by the Sea of Galilee. Born in Bethlehem and raised in Nazareth, Jesus made Capernaum His ministry headquarters. From Capernaum He would regularly walk almost four miles to the Sea of Galilee to teach or to take a boat to other villages. On this occasion, Jesus had spent the day on the shore of the Galilean Sea teaching whoever would listen about the Kingdom of God using stories of a farmer and a mustard seed. The crowd was enthralled.

At some point Jesus told His twelve closest disciples that they were going to travel by boat to the other side of the Sea to teach in other villages. Sometime during their trip, a fierce gale kicked up. These winds were not uncommon, and Jesus' disciples, many being fishermen who knew these waters well, were familiar with how life-threatening they could be. They knew that men and women had lost their lives because of the destruction these winds had caused. Believing they were going to die, the disciples became gravely fearful.

In one of the great biblical contrasts, Jesus slept while the disciples panicked. On the same boat in the same storm, the disciples were terrified, yet Jesus rested. Frustrated with His apparent ambivalence, the disciples woke Him and asked, "Do you not care that we are perishing?" (Mark 4:38).

Their question shows how little they understood about whom they were with on the boat. They had just asked the Son of God, who had left Heaven to rescue all of mankind and who had already performed many healings and miracles, *if He cares*.

What happens next is nothing short of confounding. In order to feel a measure of the fullness of the event, you have to transport yourself from wherever you are right now to being on that boat with *no knowledge* of what is going to happen. You believe you are going to die. No amount of money, talent, intelligence, or skill can help you. You are powerless and the situation is out of control. You and the other disciples wake Jesus.

Intently, you watch His every move. Everything seems to happen in slow motion. He stands up. He looks at your ragged, panicked group. His eyes are filled with some kind of confident assurance that you've never seen before, like He knows something you don't. Another wave strikes the boat. The wood groans loudly against the strain.

Then, Jesus *faces* the storm. He turns into the very thing that threatens your life and from which you're feverishly trying to invent an escape. With no fear, hesitation, or doubt, He speaks to the wind. He talks to nature!

"Hush, be still."

The wind obeys—instantly. Like a child given stern direction from a parent, the wind was put in its place. It became *perfectly* calm. The storm was gone. He spoke and the wind stopped. Your eyes move from where the wind used to be back to Jesus. Your mind races with questions, fills with confusion, and attempts to process what you just saw, as if it is possible to fully process.

Jesus' eyes move from where the wind was back to you.
"Why are you afraid? Do you still have no faith?"

Silence.

Slowly, you and the others begin looking at each other for affirmation that you're not crazy.

"Did you see what I saw?" pounds in your mind but cannot come out of your mouth. Fear from the storm is quickly replaced by fear of this wind-stopping man.

"Who then is this, that even the wind and the sea obey Him?" (Mark 4:41).

Jesus lived life in a completely different way. He is perplexing, frustrating, confusing, and mystifying. He is powerful, graceful, merciful, wise, intense, loving, caring, peaceful, joy-filled, selfless, sacrificial, generous, resolute, determined, and unstoppable.

He lived a supernaturally pragmatic life. He clearly demonstrates the reality of a spiritual, invisible-to-the-eye reality. He is empowered by the Holy Spirit, casts out demons, and performs healings that are impossible in a purely natural world. Yet, His life was very practical. He had an intentional mission. He was involved in the mess of people's lives. He did not withdraw from culture. His friends came from all walks of life. He did not dismiss issues or believe we should all just get along.

There was a rhythm and flow to His life. He was fully present in every moment and each moment seamlessly followed the one before it. How can anyone read His life and not be in awe of Him? His teachings are glorious. His way of life is secure. His love is imminently available.

His grace is perfectly given.

There is no one who compares.

None.

THE KINGDOM WAY OF LIFE

Jesus describes His way of life as the way of living in the Kingdom of God. In Mark 1:15, Jesus' first recorded sermon is given: "The time is fulfilled, the Kingdom of God is at hand; repent and believe in the Gospel."

Jesus came to re-establish the Kingdom of God on earth. God's Kingdom is His reign and rule. It is not defined by physical geography. His reign is wherever His people are. Life in God's Kingdom, seen perfectly in Jesus, is markedly different than life in the world.

At the core of Jesus' Kingdom life was deep intimacy with His Father and the Holy Spirit. He knew His Father and spent time embracing and cultivating that relationship of pure love and trust. Jesus says in John 5:19–20,

> Truly, truly I say to you, the Son can do nothing of Himself, unless it is something He sees the Father doing; for whatever the Father does, these things the Son also does in like manner. For the Father loves the Son, and shows Him all things that He Himself is doing; and the Father will show Him greater works than these, so that you will marvel.

Jesus knew His Dad. He loved His Dad and His Dad loved Him. He lived His life in a continual condition of love and acceptance.

Jesus' relationship with the Holy Spirit was the same. As we will see in Chapter 3, the prophet Isaiah declares three times that the Messiah will come and will be anointed in the Holy Spirit (Isaiah 11:1–5, 42:1–4, and 61:1–3). In Luke 4:16–21, Jesus affirmed this about Himself when He cites Isaiah 61:1–3. The Holy Spirit was in Jesus. As the indwelling presence of God in Jesus, the Spirit empowered Him, sustained Him, and was intimately with Him. In fact, Jesus and the Spirit were so intimate with each other that Paul referred to the Holy Spirit in Romans 8:9 as the Spirit, the Spirit of God, and the Spirit of Christ!

The love and trust for His Father and the Spirit led Jesus to live freely, joyfully surrendered. He lived out His faith in His Father's will by rejecting all other ways of life, even if it meant His death. Jesus did not live for Himself. He lived to bring glory to His Father (e.g., John 17:1–5). God the Father had a plan for Jesus. He sent the Spirit to empower and lead Jesus to successfully accomplish that plan. Jesus surrendered His life, embraced His Father's plan, and lived faithfully.

Deep intimacy, trust, and faithfulness are marks of Jesus' Kingdom life. As you work through this book you will come into contact with many more of the distinguishing characteristics of Jesus' life. He was a man of great depth who exemplified and taught life as God intended it to be.

JESUS' RECIPE FOR KINGDOM LIVING

How many times have you tasted some fantastic food—the moistest chocolate cake, the perfect steak, a great piece of chicken—and then asked for the recipe? "Alright, I have tasted and seen that it is good. Now, how do you make this?" You want the recipe because you do not want to have to go to the restaurant or to someone else's house. You want to make it yourself. You ask the one who cooked the meal if they will share their recipe with you. You tell them how much you *loved* their food and would love to cook it yourself and teach others how to cook it. The world has to taste this food!

The cook will say one of three things. "I do not have a recipe. I put in a little bit of this and a little bit of that." Or they will say, "I have a recipe, but it's a secret and you cannot have it."

Or they will say, "Here's the recipe. Let me teach you how to make it correctly so that you can enjoy it yourself and teach it to others!"

King David shouts an invitation to anyone who will hear him in Psalm 34:8, "O taste and see that the Lord is good; How blessed is the man who takes refuge in Him!" He invites people to taste the Lord—to experience His presence and provision for life and see that He is good. David's "taste and see" must be followed up with a recipe. "Alright, I have tasted and seen. Now what is the recipe? How do I walk with God so that I can know Him and His presence for my life?"

Jesus had a recipe for His Kingdom-living. He clearly understood how to walk with God in the reality of the world He lived in without doubt or confusion. Jesus' clarity in His walk gave Him confidence in His walk. People saw His life and said, "Who then is this, that even the wind and the sea obey Him?" Then they left everything they had to follow Him and learn His recipe for how He lived.

Jesus says in John 14:6, "I am the way, the truth, and the life; no one comes to the Father but through Me." Usually the emphasis in the passage is given on Jesus being the only way to get to Heaven and be with the Father. That is certainly, absolutely true. I see another truth in the passage as well, an equation of sorts.

Jesus says He is the way. His way, His recipe, is THE way of life. His recipe is THE recipe. Other recipes exist. People can choose other paths in life to walk. But Jesus boldly declares that His way is THE way. Then Jesus says that His way is according to THE truth. The reason His way works is because His truth is THE truth. As there are many different ways, so too there are "many" truths. Jesus says, "No." He declares that *He* is the truth. What He says and what He teaches is truth. Everything else is lies. The combination of Jesus' way and His truth is life—THE life. His way and truth is life experienced and lived in the fullness of what God the Creator and Giver of life intended.

WAY + TRUTH = LIFE

Jesus' Kingdom recipe is available to everyone. His recipe is not confidential. There are no private meetings or secret handshakes.

Jesus lived and taught in public, inviting whoever would come to learn from Him. He invited the wealthy, the poor, the immoral, the religious, the spiritual, the atheist, the Jew, the Gentile, the men, the women, and even the children to come learn His recipe for life.

His invitation included an expectation that His way would work for all those who followed Him. After He calmed the winds on the boat, Jesus rebuked His disciples: "Do you still have no faith?" However much Jesus had trained them to this point, Jesus expected it to work. Their training was sufficient to change the way they dealt with situations that confronted them.

But Jesus rebuked His disciples' lack of faith in the book of Matthew. They had little faith in God's provision (6:30). Peter questioned Jesus' ability to sustain him while he walked on water in the midst of howling winds (14:31). They were incredulous when Jesus miraculously provided food to the masses (16:8). And they were dumbstruck about their power to cast out demons (17:20).

This should be very assuring for those who follow Jesus. We should learn His way of life and expect it to work in the chaos of life. As His way equipped Him to deal with even the most uncontrollable of situations, so too should we walk in great confidence that His way of life equips us in the exact same way.

THE WAY OF REST: A KINGDOM RECIPE

In Matthew 11:28-30, Jesus gives us one of His fantastic promises:

> Come to Me, all who are weary and heavy-laden, and I will give you rest. Take My yoke upon you and learn from Me, for I am gentle and humble in heart, and you will find rest for your souls. For My yoke is easy and My burden is light.

Jesus' Kingdom way is the way of rest. He invites the weary to "learn from Me," to learn how to live a life that will produce rest. He *promises* that there is a different way to live that will produce different experiences. And He *promises* that His recipe will work!

I have named this method of walking in Jesus' Kingdom way the Way of Rest. God has always had a present experience of rest waiting for those who will walk with Him. Jeremiah 6:16 stands with Matthew 11:28–30 as another strong example of God's rest promise: "Thus says the Lord, 'Stand by the ways and see and ask for the ancient paths, Where the good way is, and walk in it; *And you will find rest for your souls*'" (emphasis added).

Similar to John 14:6 and Matthew 11:28–30, notice that God acknowledges other paths of life are available. Options exist. He encourages Israel to consider and evaluate all of them. Look for the path that produces rest. Then choose to walk in that one while rejecting all the others.

Jeremiah records the astounding, perplexing answer of Israel at the end of the verse: "But they said, 'We will not walk in it.'" They chose to reject the way of God! Consequently, although called the "chosen people of God," they did not experience the promised rest of God. They rejected God's recipe and attempted to blend different recipes. It didn't work!

So, I have named this method the Way of Rest as a way of focusing disciples on a particular promise of God that can only be supplied from Him. There is no way to rest without being intimate with the God of rest. The intent is to provide a framework that is broad enough to explain God and life and narrow enough to train in specific, daily techniques. Embracing this way will give a follower of Jesus clarity and confidence in their relationship with God.

The Way of Rest relies on five ingredients, or principles. Certainly, more principles are involved in a person's relationship with Jesus, but we can operate in these five foundational principles through which we understand everything else. These principles give us a framework whereby other truths can fit.

THE FIVE INGREDIENTS TO THE WAY OF REST:

1. We believe in **one** God who is Father, Son, and Holy Spirit.
2. We believe in **two** kingdoms in conflict.
3. We believe in **three** sources of bondage: sin, the world, and Satan.
4. We believe in **four** primary promises through Jesus alone: love, freedom, rest, and power.
5. We believe in **five** disciplines: reflecting, releasing, receiving, resisting, and responding.

This is the recipe. The Way of Rest is holistic. In other words, it covers everything a believer needs in order to be faithful to God in all things. Embracing this will position anyone to experience the intimacy and trust of Jesus' life and will produce His faithfulness. The pattern is simple but can be as complex as anyone wants it to be. This is one way of understanding how Jesus lived.

Throughout the rest of this book we're going to work through each of these truths. By the time you've finished, you will be equipped with a holistic method of walking in relationship with the Father, Son, and Holy Spirit. You will have clarity and confidence in how to BE a disciple!

RECIPE WARNINGS

As we proceed, we need to keep four realities about Jesus' recipe in mind. First, the recipe is not the substance. The paper that my recipe for chocolate cake is written on is not the substance. The paper itself doesn't taste very good! The chocolate cake that results from following the recipe is the substance! Jesus' recipe is not the substance. The substance is the relationship you have with God the Father, Son, and Holy Spirit. That is everything! A recipe—a method for walking through life— simply gives understanding for how the relationship works.

The Pharisees were a group of leading Jews in the time of Jesus. They were well known for their knowledge of the Jewish Scriptures. They spent hours and years memorizing the Scriptures and governing Israel according to them. But they made a fatal flaw in making the Scriptures the substance. On one occasion Jesus stood before them and said, "You search the Scriptures because you think that *in them* you have eternal life; it is these that testify about Me; and you are unwilling *to come to Me* so that you may have life" (John 5:39–40, emphasis added). The substance was Jesus. The substance was not the recipe. *And Jesus had life for them!*

Second, His recipe is durable. Jesus endured rejection, injustice, deceit, pain, suffering, demonic attacks, and temptation. Yet, the way He lived His life positioned Him to walk in victory. He did not simply survive. He lived a great life. The greatest proof to Jesus' way of life is His resurrection. Not even death could stop His life!

On the day of Pentecost, when the Holy Spirit first came upon the same disciples who panicked at the storm on the Sea, Peter stood and boldly preached to the masses of Jews. Acts 2:22–24 records a portion of his words:

Men of Israel, listen to these words: Jesus the Nazarene, a man attested to you by God with miracles and wonders and signs which God performed through Him in your midst, just as you yourselves know—this Man, delivered over by the predetermined plan and foreknowledge of God, you nailed to a cross by the hands of godless men and put Him to death. But God raised Him up again, putting an end to the agony of death, *since it was impossible for Him to be held in its power* (emphasis added).

Jesus' way of life empowered Him to overcome everything in life from the smallest storm to death itself. This offers us great assurance to know that there is a way to live that is strong enough to carry us through all forms of tragedy and attack we suffer, both internally and externally. For the one who embraces Jesus' way, they live and enjoy the benefit of the same beautiful certainty Jesus had on the Sea.

Third, you cannot mix recipes. Jesus' recipe was not satisfactory for only one area of His life. He did not have different ways of living for different areas of His life. In order to walk in the way of Jesus, one must walk away from all other ways, no matter what source the method came from, who taught it, or how ingrained it may be. To walk in Jesus' way is to not walk in anyone else's way.

In Jesus' promise of rest in Matthew 11:28–30, He says, "Come to Me. . . . learn from Me." One must leave everyone and everything else and learn from Him only. Throughout His ministry Jesus called people out of their ways of life to embrace Him and His way of life. Jesus once taught a group of people in a house so full that no one else could get in. Mary, his mother, and his brothers and sisters showed up and tried to get to Him. Someone in the house told Jesus that His family was outside.

Jesus responded, "My mother and My brothers are those who hear the word of God and do it" (Luke 8:21). Jesus even called His own family out of their ways to follow Him. Jesus had no exceptions or special treatments. To walk with Jesus is to abandon all other teachings and recipes.

Fourth, the recipe has no order! This is both glorious and frustrating. Jesus used no laid-out, systematic way of teaching people His recipe. In His maturity He taught what His disciples needed. He did not sit with them and say, "This is first, second, third, and fourth." His recipe did not require the ingredients to be added in order.

I believe He did not have an order because we would easily make our lives about His recipe and not about Him. It is so tempting to believe, "Okay, now that I have the recipe I'm good!" NO! The recipe is not the substance. The Father, Son, and Holy Spirit are the substance. Jesus did not need an order because He was so confident in His recipe that He was freed to teach as needed.

Think about an area of your life where you have confidence. Maybe it's cooking, parenting, managing, selling, building, or harvesting. If you had to train someone else to do what you do, would you need an order? Or, based on your maturity and confidence, would you be freed to teach as needed?

We want to give you a recipe you can embrace and use as your way of walking in relationship with the Father, Son, and Holy Spirit. You are certainly able to tweak our recipe and make it your own or use ours as an example and build your own. Whatever you do, get a recipe that gives you clarity and confidence in Jesus and produces the promises of God.

We are trapped in the "tortured middle," the horrible place between returning to the world and fully surrendering to Jesus. We know we cannot deny Jesus and go back to the world. However, we are not experiencing the life we read about in the Bible or hear about at church. So we either give up or try harder by reading more, serving more, or giving more. Yet none of it works. The great news for you is that hope is closer than you think. More than likely you already have some very good ingredients to your recipe. You may need correction, development, or even a fresh start in some areas. But you're close. Don't let the enemy discourage you anymore.

A second group of people are those who are strong in the Lord. The fruit of your lives bears witness to the work of the Holy Spirit conforming you into the image of Jesus. However, you do not have a clear way in which you walk. If someone asked you how you walk with the Lord, you would respond with something like, "I do a little bit of this and a little bit of that." What you do works, and it works well for you, but it does not transfer easily to others. Making disciples is harder for you than it needs to be because you do not have clarity in what you do. For those in this group, developing a clear way of walking with Jesus will be a matter of organizing what you're already doing.

For those who are newer to the faith and just learning what it means to walk with the Father, Son, and Holy Spirit, you are in a great, great place! You have been given a wonderful opportunity to learn a holistic recipe for walking with Jesus that will give you the foundation you need for the rest of your life.

ONE LAST WARNING

Before moving on to Chapter 2, let's return to the Kingdom of God and emphasize the separation that happens when a person becomes a follower of Jesus. So much frustration, confusion, and continued oppression can happen in a person's life simply because they're trying to mix the way of Jesus and the way of the world. It doesn't work.

Graciously and mercifully, Jesus will continue to challenge the ways that you live and what you believe. Life will take you to the middle of the Sea of Galilee and your beliefs will be exposed. Jesus loves you and wants you for Himself. He wants you to trust in Him and His ways in totality. You can waste many years and unnecessarily suffer much anxiety and fear because you're holding on to ways of this world. Let me encourage you as God deals with the path of life you're on to rest in Him, trust Him, and follow Him.

ASLEEP IN THE STORM: CHAPTER WORK

Begin this work in prayer. Spend time in prayer considering the strength of your intimacy with the Lord. Reflect on the remarkable life of Jesus. Is there anyone else you want to be like? Is He worth your complete loyalty? As you observe His life, what do you see? Thank your Father for the life and example of His Son. Ask the Holy Spirit to show you everything He has for you as you work through these questions.

1. What are the most remarkable aspects of Jesus' life that you have discovered?

2. What are the most challenging aspects of Jesus' life?

3. What has been happening in your life that has brought you to a place where you're ready to leave the way of the world and walk in the way of Jesus?

4. On a scale of one to ten, with ten being the strongest, how confident are you in your relationship with Jesus? (It may be helpful to answer this question by considering how confident you are to teach someone else to do what you do in your relationship with the Lord. This can be a great way of determining your clarity in what you do.) What are the strengths of your faith? What are your weaknesses? Based on Chapter 1, what are some of the gaps you have?

5. Are there storms you're dealing with today? What are they? How does Mark 4:31–35 equip you to deal with them in a Kingdom Way?

6. Take some time and write out the five ingredients of the Way of Rest.

BE

THE WAY OF REST

2: THE PUZZLE BOX TOP

Have you ever tried to build a puzzle without the top of the box? The agony! You have no clarity on what the puzzle is. You have a mess of pieces with no idea how they all fit or if any are missing. You see clumps of similar color and guess they go together but cannot tell if they do or how they relate to other clumps of color. Can you still build the puzzle?

Sure. Many people do. But how much unnecessary frustration and exhaustion are you going to deal with? Do you want to build the puzzle with the uncertainty of not knowing if you have all the pieces? Do you want to continuously learn from your mistakes because you keep trying to fit pieces together that do not go together?

Many people quit. It's just too confusing and they have other things less complicated to deal with. There are other things that seem much simpler and this should not be so hard. How much would the box top *shed light* on the puzzle? How much more would you be equipped to succeed? How much would clarity give you confidence?

Jesus lived with pristine clarity on the Big Picture of the world. He knew the box top of all creation. He knew all the pieces and how they fit. He did not trip over things, and He was not tripped by things He could not see. He was never surprised or caught off guard. Because of what He believed about the world, He never feared the uncontrollable or was taunted by the unknown. "What-ifs" had *no* power in His life. *There was nothing He was going to be confronted with that His beliefs did not equip Him to deal with.* Can you imagine living like that? No fear of the unknown or the uncontrollable. Amazing. His clarity about the world was a powerful tool that equipped Him to navigate the "chaos" and "unpredictability" of life.

We need His clarity!

To walk in Jesus' way is to walk in Jesus' world. To believe in Jesus is to believe in Jesus' world. He invites people to walk with Him in His world. His God is our God. His beliefs are our beliefs. His enemies are our enemies. His world is our world.

To understand Jesus' world, to get His clarity, we have a diagram in the Way of Rest called the Eph 1. The Eph 1 is largely based on Ephesians 1:18–2:10. It is the puzzle box top that gives definition and perspective to the puzzle and provides insight into how the pieces fit together.

The Eph 1 identifies all the persons and forces at work in creation and how they relate to each other. Learning the Eph 1 will give you the clarity Jesus had, which is the clarity you've been longing for. The Eph 1 will give you something you can continually come back to and work from. As you progress in the diagram, you will learn how to take one piece out of the Eph 1, examine it, meditate on it, be blessed by it, and then put it back in the puzzle.

In addition to helping connect pieces, the Eph 1 also helps keep faith balanced. Commonly, followers of Jesus get caught up in one section of the puzzle. They have many pieces in that area of the puzzle properly placed, but the rest of the puzzle is missing.

For example, a person is strong in their knowledge about the end times, but balance is missing in their Trinitarian theology. Another person may be strong in understanding the providence of God, but their knowledge of spiritual warfare is lacking. The Eph 1 diagram provides us a way to see many different aspects of Jesus' world, which helps to keep our faith strong in all areas.

The Eph 1 diagram has six steps. Read through the following passage first. Walk through the diagram. Then come back and read the passage again.

I pray that the eyes of your heart may be enlightened, so that you will know what is the hope of His calling, what are the riches of the glory of His inheritance in the saints, and what is the surpassing greatness of His power toward us who believe.

These are in accordance with the working of the strength of His might which He brought about in Christ, when He raised Him from the dead and seated Him at His right hand in the heavenly places, far above all rule and authority and power and dominion, and every name that is named, not only in this age but also in the one to come.

And He put all things in subjection under His feet, and gave Him as head over all things to the church, which is His body, the fullness of Him who fills all in all.

And you were dead in your trespasses and sins, in which you formerly walked according to the course of this world, according to the prince of the power of the air, of the spirit that is now working in the sons of disobedience. Among them we too all formerly lived in the lusts of our flesh, indulging the desires of the flesh and of the mind, and were by nature children of wrath, even as the rest.

But God, being rich in mercy, because of His great love with which He loved us, even when we were dead in our transgressions, made us alive together with Christ (by grace you have been saved), and raised us up with Him, and seated us with Him in the heavenly places in Christ Jesus, so that in the ages to come He might show the surpassing riches of His grace in kindness toward us in Christ Jesus.

For by grace you have been saved through faith; and that not of yourselves, it is the gift of God; not as a result of works, so that no one may boast. For we are His workmanship, created in Christ Jesus for good works, which God prepared beforehand so that we would walk in them (Eph. 1:18–2:10).

Diagram 1: God the Father, Son, and Holy Spirit

Diagram 1 depicts one God who is Father, Son, and Holy Spirit and shows that:

1. God exists before time.

2. God exists in community. He is relational.

3. The spiritual has priority over the physical.

The white space in Diagram 1 demonstrates that in the beginning, before God created anything, He was. He is outside of time and Lord of time. He is not subject to anything or anyone.

God existed in perfect relationship with Himself as Father, Son, and Holy Spirit. Therefore, His essence is relational.

His essence is also spiritual. Before there is anything physical there is the one spiritual being, God. Consequently, the spiritual has priority over the physical even today.

ANGELS

Diagram 2: Creation

Diagram 2 depicts God's work in creation and shows that:

1. Everything is made by God—angels, universe, and man.

2. God moves everything according to His will. (The arrow symbolizes the will of God.)

3. Man has been made in the image of God.

4. Man has been made for a relationship with the Father, Son, and Holy Spirit.

5. Obedience is the demonstration of love.

At some point God the Father decided to build creation. The Son and the Spirit carry out His will in such a way that all three persons of the Trinity perform different functions in the creating.

Angels, the physical universe, and man are all created by God. Man stands out as the unique creation of God as the only one created in the image of God. God made man to be in relationship with Him, to be blessed by Him, and to be faithful to Him.

God places man in the Garden of Eden and commands him not to eat from one of the trees called the Tree of Knowledge of Good and Evil. God puts man in a situation where his love would be demonstrated through his faithful obedience to God's Word.

God makes all of creation in six days. On the sixth day Scripture teaches that God saw all that He had made and it was "very good" (Genesis 1:31).

Diagram 3: Rebellion, War, and Bondage

Depicting two Kingdoms in conflict and three sources of bondage, Diagram 3 shows:

1. The rebellion of Lucifer and the creation of his demonic kingdom.
2. The war between the kingdoms.
3. The world ruled by the enemy.
4. The fall of man.
5. The bondage that has come from sin, the world, and Satan.

Sometime after the "very good" of Genesis 1:31 and the appearance of the serpent in Genesis 3:1, a rebellion broke out in the heavenlies. Wanting glory for himself, Lucifer rebelled against God. Convincing one-third of the angels to leave with him, Lucifer, now known as Satan, established his demonic kingdom.

What began in the heavenlies came to Earth as Satan disguised himself as a serpent and tempted God's created woman, Eve. Adam and Eve both fell in temptation and sinned against God.

Consequently, Satan took dominion of the world, and sin entered life, corrupting all of God's creation. Satan, the world, and sin now actively war against God and man.

What God created for life was now at war against Him and produced death.

Diagram 4: Jesus

Diagram 4 depicts the story of the four promises of God and shows that:

1. The Son of God came in the flesh as Jesus in fulfillment of the Father's promise.
2. Jesus lived a life filled with the Spirit.
3. Jesus re-established the Kingdom of God on earth.
4. His death is a sufficient sacrifice for our sins.
5. He is raised over all rulers and authorities and sits at the right hand of the Father making the promises of God available to anyone who will believe in Him.

God has always been and will always be faithful. He will not allow the enemy victory.

Therefore, according to His promise, God the Father sent His Son full of the Holy Spirit to earth. Jesus was born because God the Father was faithful to His word.

Jesus lived a sinless life through the power of the Holy Spirit to re-establish the Kingdom of God. In His life, death, and resurrection Jesus overcame sin, the world, and Satan.

He is then raised far above all rulers and powers and is eternally enthroned at the right hand of the Father.

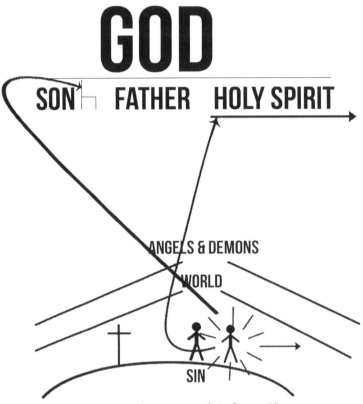

Diagram 5: Salvation and Life in Christ

Diagram 5 depicts the four promises—love, freedom, rest, and power—and the five disciplines—reflecting, releasing, receiving, resisting, and responding—and shows how:

1. We surrender and begin walking with the Father, Son, and Holy Spirit.
2. We walk in the promises of God by grace through the work of Jesus.
3. We are raised and seated with Jesus at the right hand of the Father.
4. We practice the five disciplines.
5. We walk with others.

Every person lives in the war, subject to the powers of Satan, the world, and sin and separated from the perfect love of the Father, Son, and Holy Spirit. Through the spreading of the Gospel, people are given opportunities to surrender their lives and begin walking with Jesus in the promises of God.

Upon surrendering to Jesus, a person is filled with the promised Holy Spirit, transferred into the Kingdom of God, made a child of God, raised and seated with Christ in the heavenlies, and made an heir of the promises of God. All of this is done by grace through Jesus Christ.

In a new Christian life, a believer learns to practice new disciplines that align with his or her new beliefs and new position. In that new life, the new believer gathers together with other followers of Jesus and the Holy Spirit creates, sustains, and grows communities of faith who go to make disciples of others.

ANGELS

Diagram 6: The End

Diagram 6 depicts the final results:

1. Judgment
2. Re-creation

Finally, God the Father sends Jesus again to completely fulfill His promise of total victory and restoration. Everyone is judged. The faithful pass into eternal life in the presence of God. The unfaithful, both man and demonic, are cast into eternal damnation where they will suffer.

In accordance with His word, God remakes creation without sin or the possibility of sin. The faithful live in eternity, enjoying the presence of God.

EPH 1 CONCLUSION

Through the Eph 1 we see the world Jesus lived in. Jesus did not live His life in seclusion. His way was not void of struggle and war. He did not try to escape culture or avoid the chaos of life. He lived in dynamic intimacy with the triune God. He showed us the reality of, and the relationship between, the supernatural and the natural. He lived at rest in the midst of it all. In many ways, He never left the messy manger where He was born. The Eph 1 is a simple tool that clarifies the world Jesus lived in and taught.

Spend some time in the Eph 1. Draw it over and over again. Return to it regularly and allow the Holy Spirit to further clarify life through it. Oftentimes He will use the Eph 1 to show you aspects of your faith that are being attacked or areas that He wants to develop.

Living Jesus' Kingdom way requires living in Jesus' world.

THE PUZZLE BOX TOP: CHAPTER WORK

Begin your work by meditating on God's story in the Eph 1. Allow the Holy Spirit to take you, in His timing, through each portion. As you are brought to the end, bless the Lord for His wisdom, His love, and His plan.

1. What areas represented in the diagram are most underdeveloped in you?

2. What areas are you strongest in?

3. What areas does the Eph 1 clarify for you?

4. What effect does God existing in spirit before anything physical was created have on your beliefs about the nature of creation? What does it show you about what is important in life?

5. How do you think Satan and his army felt as they watched Jesus ascend and sit at the right hand of His Father?

6. What impact does Jesus being raised far above all rule and principality have on your authority today?

7. Read 1 John 5:19–20. How do you see the effect of Satan ruling over all creation?

8. Read 1 John 2:15–17. What are the messages of the world that you struggle with?

9. Read 2 Corinthians 5:17. What does the Scripture mean when it says that you have been made a new creation in Christ?

Continue to draw the Eph 1 on your own. The more you practice it the more clarity you will receive through it.

3: ORGANICS

Jesus lived with an awe-inspiring rhythm. Despite the enormity of His life and mission, you just do not see Him straining to get through His days. He is like water freely moving over rocks. He is like a married couple, deeply in love, moving in perfect rhythm on the dance floor. Jesus' life flowed. And it isn't that He had no issues. He had plenty, and to a degree that neither you nor I will endure. Nevertheless, He moved gracefully, intently, and powerfully through His days. He lived in the fullness of every moment. He did not shut Himself down emotionally or live with some version of a hands-off approach to life. He did not simply let things roll off His back. Remarkably, He was perfectly, fully vested in every moment.

When you watch an expert at what they do, what they do appears effortless. An expert downhill skier makes skiing look so easy you think you could do it. A professional chef makes an excellent dish that tastes fantastic. What happens when you try to emulate them? You try skiing and wreck. You try cooking and start fires! Jesus was THE life expert. He was smooth. He made it look easy. In the last chapter we understood that part of His ease came from seeing the world correctly. The light was on and He saw where all the furniture was located. He never stumbled around trying to feel His way.

In this chapter, we're going to work through organics: the connection among beliefs, practices, and experiences. Jesus had a seamless connection between His beliefs, practices, and experiences. There was no disconnect, compartmentalization, missing pieces, or confusion. Like water moving from a root to a vine to a branch and then producing fruit, Jesus' beliefs flowed fluidly to His practices, which easily yielded fruit.

Have you ever driven a car that's out of alignment? You hold the steering wheel straight, but the car veers to the left or right. How does that happen? Your steering column and your wheels are not in alignment! If you are out of alignment and continue holding the wheel straight, you're going to get into a wreck. Many people's lives are wrecks, even Christians' lives, because their beliefs and practices are out of alignment. Through organics we're going to discover our alignment issues.

BRANCHES AND SHEEP

Jesus trains His disciples about the power of an aligned life using the image of a vine and a branch. In John 15:5 Jesus says, "I am the vine, you are the branches. He who abides in Me and I in him will bear much fruit. For apart from Me you can do nothing." Let's break this down according to beliefs, practices, and experiences.

Let's take a deeper look at Jesus' vine/branch analogy through our organic lens of beliefs, practices, and results. At the level of belief, He is a vine and we are branches. As the vine, He takes on all the responsibilities of the vine. He is the provider. As branches, we are to take on all the responsibilities of the branch. We are receivers. We must believe that He can and will supply all that we need at all times in everything. We must believe that our role is to receive what the vine has for us. We must believe that all we are is a branch.

If we believe these things, then appropriate practices will *naturally* follow. If we believe in the vine/branch, then we will by nature abide. To abide is to remain in something. A branch is designed to remain in, to continually be connected to, a vine. Nothing is more central to the life of the branch than its connection to the vine. The branch wants to be an expert at abiding in the vine. Therefore, if we believe we are a branch, then we will abide naturally and joyfully. Abiding is what we have been designed to do.

Consequently, according to Jesus, if we believe and practice the vine/branch relationship, then we will experience abundant fruit in our lives, and we will bear much fruit. When God Himself abides in us and we in Him, we will be abundant. We will clearly and consistently bear fruit upon fruit upon fruit!

A man I know loves the Lord. He has walked with God for years. He could defend the faith well and sought opportunities to do so. However, his practices were always inconsistent. Regularly getting into the Word of God was a chore. Because he believed many of the right things, it took a while to discover what was happening in his life. We found that while his beliefs were correct, they were incomplete and out-of-order. He had a strong relationship with Jesus but did not understand the Spirit well. And his devotion to his children often competed with his devotion to the Lord. His inconsistency in his practices disappeared when we addressed his beliefs and he experienced abundant, natural fruit for the first time in his faith.

RESULTS

PRACTICES

BELIEFS

Every one of us has a system of beliefs and practices. Through our relationship with Jesus, He changes our systems. He transforms our beliefs (Romans 12:2) and practices to produce His life in us.

With this understanding of abundance, we are now ready to explore various conditions of our beliefs, practices, and results that keep us from Jesus' promised abundance. Then we will learn from Jesus the foundational beliefs and practices of the Way of Rest.

BELIEFS

Beliefs are the truths that define life for us. They can move from simple to complex, and as the foundation of our lives they are very powerful. Jesus says, "For God so loved the world that He gave His only Son that whoever believes in Him shall not perish but will have eternal life" (John 3:16). The impact of truly believing this one statement is staggering. Accepting this as true will determine the trajectory of a person's life. Beliefs form the lens through which we interpret and understand life. They are foundational.

Unfortunately, not all of our beliefs are accurate. Often, they're a mix of six different conditions: incorrect, inconsistent, incomplete, out-of-order, wounded, or bound. The lines among these are certainly blurred, but the distinctions can help to bring needed clarity.

No matter how faithful and sincere our practices are, when they are placed on top of beliefs that are in one of these conditions, we will not experience the rest and promises of God in our lives. As disciples, we want our beliefs to be clear. As we go to make disciples, we want to observe the belief condition of those we disciple so that we can train them appropriately.

INCORRECT BELIEFS

Incorrect beliefs occur when we accept concepts as truth that are, in fact, lies. An example of incorrect beliefs is found in the counsel Job's friends gave to him throughout the book of Job. Job's friends tried to convince him that he must have done something wrong to have experienced the loss he suffered. They adhered to the concept that everything that happens in life is either a blessing because of good works or retribution for bad works. This belief is based on a lie that denies God's grace and mercy and misunderstands His sovereignty.

When we make a mistake and continue to beat ourselves up for that mistake, we're allowing the same incorrect belief to guide our path. This practice of beating ourselves up is based on an incorrect belief that we deserved what we got or that God is mad at us. Therefore, we believe we will become holier if we suffer longer. This is an example of a lie based on an incorrect belief.

INCONSISTENT BELIEFS

Inconsistent beliefs occur when we believe God is faithful in some things but not in others, and when we believe God is faithful sometimes but not all the time. A person believes God is faithful in his or her finances in the morning, but by the afternoon he or she has forgotten God's faithfulness and is filled with anxiety. Another person believes God is faithful in his or her marriage but not his or her career. God is not sometimes, or in some things, faithful. He is faithful all the time and in all things. Inconsistent beliefs are notorious contributors to a confused faith.

INCOMPLETE BELIEFS

Incomplete beliefs occur when a person does not believe everything Scripture says. We see incomplete belief predominantly occur in two areas in the United States: Trinitarian balance and spiritual warfare. We will cover these in-depth later.

Simply, Trinitarian balance is the need to live in an appropriate relationship with each person of the Trinity: the Father, Son, and Holy Spirit. Spiritual warfare is engaging the demonic in the war of the Kingdoms. An example was given in Chapter 1 of a woman warring against the negativity in her mind. Her attack could easily have been demonic. Had she not believed in spiritual warfare, she would have been left defenseless. Inadequacy in Trinitarian balance, spiritual warfare, and other principles are examples of incomplete beliefs.

OUT-OF-ORDER BELIEFS

This condition is marked by an inaccurate prioritizing of belief in Jesus in our lives. Even though a person believes in Christ, his or her belief in Christ is not their number-one priority. Jesus says that we are to love the Lord so much that we "hate" our fathers, mothers, brothers, and sisters. We are to have no other gods but God Himself. God is a jealous God. We can study the Bible all we want, but God must be first in our hearts or we will not succeed in our belief.

WOUNDED BELIEFS

Wounded beliefs are those beliefs a person has because of events he or she has suffered. Wounded beliefs are a prevalent force in our belief system. Recognizing the wounds we have and their effects is critically important. These wounds not only interfere with our beliefs but also can lead to incorrect, inconsistent, or incomplete beliefs.

I met a woman who said to me, "If you ask me to give my life to God or to the Spirit, I will do so now. If you ask me to give my life to the Father or to Jesus, I will never do it because I will not trust my life into the hands of another man again." Her beliefs have been deeply affected by her wounds.

BOUND BELIEFS

Beliefs can also be bound. All or portions of our beliefs can certainly be held in bondage by demonic spirits. The apostle Paul wrote in 2 Corinthians 4:3–4, "And even if our gospel is veiled, it is veiled to those who are perishing, in whose case the god of this world has blinded the minds of the unbelieving so that they might not see the light of the gospel of the glory of Christ, who is the image of God." This passage indicates that the evil demon has veiled belief in Christ. As a result, those whose beliefs have been bound are perishing.

Additionally, in 2 Timothy 2:24–26, Paul trains Timothy saying, "The Lord's bond-servant must not be quarrelsome, but be kind to all, able to teach, patient when wronged, with gentleness correcting those who are in opposition, if perhaps God may grant them repentance leading to the knowledge of the truth, and they may come to their senses and escape from the snare of the devil, *having been held captive by him to do his will*" (emphasis added). Paul is trying to show Timothy that the devil is a powerful force that can blind us from our beliefs.

When a person's beliefs are incorrect, inconsistent, incomplete, out-of-order, wounded, or bound, then no matter how consistent or sincere the practices, that person will not get the results Jesus promised. Such people may find themselves in church or reading their Bibles, believing those promised results must be for everyone else. They may find themselves trying everything harder and longer, or they may give up in their beliefs altogether, figuring that there's something fundamentally wrong with them.

Through organics, we can show that their insufficiency is not at the level of practice but rather at the level of their beliefs. Organics helps people discover the reality of what's going on in their spirits. Our goal as we sit at the feet of Jesus is to allow Him to clarify our beliefs for us and others. As we understand our beliefs and remove inaccuracies, we're ready to put those beliefs into practice.

PRACTICES

Jesus has specific ways He wants us to practice our beliefs. Jesus' disciples understood this. They came to Jesus and asked Him to teach them how to pray. Jesus gave them the Lord's Prayer. He did not say to them, "Eh, it doesn't matter what you pray as long as you pray." No. Jesus gave them specific words based on specific themes. Through the Lord's Prayer, He trained His followers in the practice of prayer. Not only did Jesus teach the importance of prayer, but He also showed its importance. Jesus lived a disciplined life. In Mark 1:35, we read how Jesus regularly drew away to be by Himself with His Father. The text says, "In the early morning, while it was still dark, Jesus got up, and left the house, and went away to a secluded place, and was praying there."

In the Sermon on the Mount, Jesus instructed his followers to reject the "righteousness," of the Pharisees. Jesus went on to tell his followers on the Mount that there is a correct way to practice faith. In John 5:20, Jesus practices receiving direction from His Father, "For the Father loves the Son, and shows Him all things that He Himself is doing; and the Father will show Him greater works than these so that you will marvel." In John 5:39–40, He rebukes the way the Pharisees read the Scriptures. He regularly corrected their interpretive methodologies. The Holy Spirit in Luke 4:1 provides direction for Jesus. Luke 4:1–13 demonstrates Jesus' practice of Scripture study and memory.

Teachings on the correct practices of our faith are not limited to Jesus. The Apostle Paul writes in Philippians 4:9, "The things you have learned and received and heard and seen in me, practice these things, and the God of peace will be with you." He wrote this after giving techniques in prayer to deal with anxiety in Philippians 4:4–7 and techniques for reflection in verse 8. In another place he says, "Imitate me." Not only did Paul tell us to practice and imitate, but Paul's life was also an example to others. Paul's writings are filled with technique-training for life in Christ.

Paul is not alone. All of Jesus' disciples taught specific techniques in their writings. Peter gives an excellent word for technique-training in 1 Peter 5:6–11. James' words in James 1:2–18 on trials and 4:7 on spiritual warfare are powerful. John's exhortation in 1 John 2:15–17 is equally strong.

The practices of our faith are not limited to the New Testament. Isaiah 58 is one of the pillar texts for fasting. Joshua 1 and Psalm 1 both give exhortation in meditation. Deuteronomy 6 stands out in Scripture memory. Both the Old Testament and the New Testament teach the importance of properly practicing our beliefs.

As we consider our own practices, we will be better able to see how those we're investing in practice the faith and help them mature as disciples. It will not be unusual to find practices that are consistent but incorrect, imbalanced, and/or obligatory.

CONSISTENT BUT INCORRECT

A person prays all the time but doesn't see any fruit from his or her prayers. A person studies the Word regularly but rarely hears from the Lord. A person meditates but has no transformation. Consistency is not the issue. Rather the person has not been trained in proper technique. In this case, we must avoid the error that the "right" word exists; however, a technique does exist for success, so we need to re-evaluate the technique or possibly the beliefs. Proper techniques will be discussed in later chapters of this book.

INCONSISTENT

When the Psalmist writes in Psalm 23, "The Lord is my Shepherd, I shall not want," he was not describing an occasional relationship. He was describing a state of being where the Shepherd leads and the sheep follow. If I believe this, then my practices will follow. Inconsistent practices usually come from beliefs that are incorrectly prioritized. Although we may believe in the Father, Son, and Holy Spirit, God is not our first priority.

OBLIGATORY

These kinds of practices are brutal. Such people practice their faith out of a sense of obligation or fear. They believe, "I guess I should read my Bible." Obligatory practices are suffocating joy-killers. Jesus does not want us to do anything for Him out of obligation. We joyfully practice our faith as a continual response to His love, presence, and work in our lives.

IMBALANCED

Imbalanced practices are particularly dangerous because they can give the illusion that you're doing what you're "supposed to be doing." For example, a person studies the Bible regularly but never engages in spiritual warfare. Another person continually sings to the Lord but rarely opens the Bible. Another person spends his or her time in devotionals but never reads the Scripture itself. Another person constantly serves but never sits still in the presence of the Lord. We need to be fully engaged in all of the practices of our faith.

As we discern the way those we're investing in practice, we may need to speak about some of these four conditions in their lives. After listening, we may say something like, "Your practices may be inconsistent." Or, "You do well in Bible study, but we need to train more in spiritual warfare." Through organics we can help them see the relationship between their inconsistency and results. The Holy Spirit is using us to connect the dots!

In the Way of Rest, we train in five specific practices:

1. Reflecting
2. Releasing
3. Receiving
4. Resisting
5. Responding

As I studied the life of Jesus and wrestled with how He could live His life as a "non-anxious" presence, I noticed that He continually exercised these five practices. Therefore, we train people in these specific techniques. Our goal is to help each person experience God's promises for his or her life in such a way that he or she can go out and confidently train others to do the same. We want our people to be able to say with Paul, "The things you have learned and received and heard and seen in me, practice these things, and the God of peace will be with you" (Philippians 4:9).

RESULTS

Again, Jesus says in the parable of the sower in Mark 4:1–20 that the seed which falls on good soil will bear fruit, "thirty, sixty, and a hundredfold." If the soil (the condition of the heart) is right, it will bear fruit. When the Word, which is certainly good, is sewn successfully the results will be successful. When our beliefs are clear and our practices are consistent, we will have abounding stories of our Father's presence, movement, and revelation. Life in Christ will be LIFE in Christ.

Results are important to God. When Jesus said, "Blessed are the poor in spirit" in Matthew 5:3, He was not referring to blessings in Heaven when a person dies. He was referring to the availability of blessings in that day. He was not referring to the poor in spirit being blessed because they're now millionaires. He spoke to something much deeper and more substantive. He was speaking about daily results in these people's lives.

The importance of results to God is easily seen in Jesus Himself. Jesus did not come and suffer and die so that people could memorize a new set of facts. He came to change lives. He came to give people a new daily experience of life in Him. He says in John 7:38, "He who believes in Me, as the Scripture said, 'From his innermost being will flow rivers of living water.'" Unfortunately, many people are unsuccessful in their results. In these individuals we have found six different types of unproductive responses.

RESULT-DEFINED

A person defines him- or herself by the results of his or her life. They identify themselves as a success or failure based on a history of events. This is a terrible condition, as the root of it is unstable and easily disturbed. In this a person's overall well-being is determined by their ability to get results. These people are always exhausted. There is no joy.

INHIBITED

For a variety of reasons a person is afraid or unwilling to allow him- or herself to feel great. There is an emotional dullness.

HAPPY

A person believes the prosperity gospel or some version of it. He or she believes that everything is always great, and all we have to do is smile or claim a verse and God will make everything wonderful.

PERSONALITY RESULTS

This is an interesting condition produced by a person's "natural" personality. Someone is by nature an optimist or a pessimist. They will stubbornly declare, "This is just who I am." This cuts off dependence upon God. Often, the circumstances of a person's life will exhaust their natural abilities, and they will not know how to deal with the situation. Additionally, personality results prevent people from transformational ministry because a natural optimist cannot convert a natural pessimist.

HOPELESS

These people have experienced continual disappointment so they have consigned themselves to hopelessness as a condition. Manifestations of this circumstance will be obvious.

DEMONIZED

These individuals may be dealing with various degrees of demonization. Even stories heard from Christians may be the result of demonic activity in their lives. You must consider this a strong, viable option for the condition of those you are discipling. For many of us, demons and demonization are difficult and uncertain topics. When they are soberly addressed and clearly explained in light of the overall reality of God and the condition of the world, then hopefully we can work our way to truth. We referenced one way demonic activity works in Chapter 1 and showed the ease with which a follower of Jesus can overcome their schemes. We will discuss their abilities and methods and our power over them in following chapters.

For successful results, the Way of Rest utilizes four primary promises of God for our lives today:

1. Love
2. Freedom
3. Rest
4. Power

God has given us other promises, but we are going to use these four as the foundational promises upon which we enjoy all of the other promises. As we go to make disciples, we will use these promises as barometers by which we can discern the condition of a person's relationship with God. In the same way we can discern the conditions of a person's marriage, family, and careers, we can discern the condition of a person's relationship with God. If they are not operating in these promises, then we know an issue exists either in beliefs or practices.

Jesus wants us to experience Him, His work, and His power in our lives. We should expect and look for results, and we should use our results as a way of evaluating the condition of our faith. Results can be difficult if they're misunderstood. Properly understood, they become great barometers of our relationship with God. As we go to make disciples, we will mostly begin in the area of the results and experiences of people's lives. God will use them as windows to deeper issues of belief and practice, so that as we believe that we are the branch to Jesus' vine and practice abiding, we will experience abundant fruit. As we believe that God is the Shepherd and we are the sheep that practice following Him, we will experience His leadership. As we believe that the Holy Spirit is our power and practice exercising His power, we will experience His victory. As we believe that we live at war against sin, the world, and Satan, and we practice warfare, we will experience breakthrough. As we believe God speaks to us today and we practice being still in His presence, we will know His voice.

RESULTS AND EVANGELISM

Most of us do not readily share our faith in Jesus because we do not have regular, powerful stories of God moving. Therefore, most of us do not believe our lives are all that enviable. Subsequently, I have to ask myself, "What is so great about my life that I would want to share with someone else how to live what I am living?" Consequently, we do not share our faith.

God intends that our experiences of Him will fuel our sharing about Him. In Paul's list of the armor of God in Ephesians 6:10–20, he teaches that our feet are to be fitted with the "Gospel of Peace." That means we are to have peace. We experience biblical, God-promised peace as the normal condition of our lives. Evangelism, then, is offering to others the peace, hope, love and power that I'm already living.

Jesus heals a leper in Mark 1. He commands the leper to silence, but the leper is so changed that he tells everyone about Jesus. He was not forced. Rather, his evangelism was a product of his encounter with Jesus. That encounter changed his beliefs and made necessary practicing something he had never done before: MISSIONS!

CONNECTING THE EPH 1 AND ORGANICS

Now that we understand the organic nature of beliefs, practices, and results, we need to add the Eph 1 diagram so that we can see the whole picture. These two create a framework that will help us as we make disciples who make disciples. At appropriate times in our discipleship, we will draw the Eph 1 diagram asking our disciples if they truly, deeply believe the truths given. His or her response will help us know in what direction we need to go. Many areas of bondage, confusion, incompletion, and weakness will be exposed. We may use completely different words, narrowing in on only certain aspects or broadening to cover the big picture depending on who we are discipling. As we walk through this, the Holy Spirit is speaking to us and to our disciples, revealing what needs to be revealed.

As beliefs are clarified, practices will begin to fall in line. A disciple's practice of spiritual warfare naturally develops as their belief in two kingdoms in conflict deepens. A disciple's practice of forgiveness matures as he or she reflects more and more on the perfect love that the Father, Son, and Holy Spirit have for them.

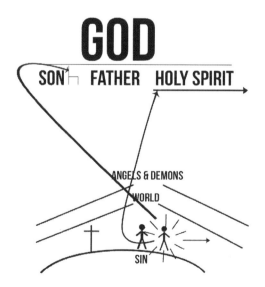

As beliefs clarify and practices become increasingly consistent, a disciple will begin to experience the promised fruit in the results of their lives. Anxiety and fear are replaced with freedom and rest. Exhaustion is replaced with divine power. Chaos is replaced with order. Darkness is replaced with light. Combining the Eph 1 and organics will make discipling people easier. Discipling will not be easy, but it can be easier.

A brother in the Lord has wrestled with fear. He believes strongly in the Lord. He has recently opened his faith to embrace an active relationship with all three persons of the Trinity. However, he feels like something is still not right as he is beset with fear. As we talked, we discovered his issues came from his practices.

He believes. However, he does not regularly sit still in the presence of God and reflect on His love. This brother's practice has been limited to a quick prayer in the morning with his wife, which is usually focused on the family and work. He rarely spends time focusing on God and himself. We trained him in some new techniques that Jesus uses to be still in the Lord. He is excitedly using these new exercises and experiencing powerful results.

CONCLUSION

Man operates organically and he relates to Jesus organically. Nothing is forced. The results of our lives are a natural product of what we believe and how we practice. When we come to faith in Christ, He changes our beliefs and our practices. This combination changes the results of our lives. People walking with Jesus will have regular stories of their relationship with Him. They will not be bothered when asked, "How is your relationship with the Lord?" They will find themselves asking others the same. They will be blessed with thirty, sixty, or one-hundred-fold growth with daily stories of the Spirit moving.

As a disciple, we want to understand our own organics. Are our beliefs, practices, and results in alignment? Are we experiencing the results God promises us and Jesus secured for us? As we make disciples, we will always be working through organics, either in the background or through direct discussion. Are the issues your disciple is dealing with a belief problem, a practice problem, or some mix of both? The Eph 1 and organics are powerful tools for discernment and in leading others to healing and maturity in their relationship with God.

ORGANICS: CHAPTER WORK

Begin your work in this chapter in prayer. Thank your Father for the understanding He has given you. He wants you to have life! Alignment issues can be major, "hidden" hindrances.

1. Read Psalm 23:1 and write out the following using the work we did in John 15:5 as a template:

Beliefs:

Practices:

Experiences:

2. What should believing each aspect of the Eph 1 have on your practices?

3. What is the condition of alignment among your beliefs, practices, and results? What is your biggest alignment issue?

4. What are the steps God is leading you to take to realign your organics?

5. How do you see your alignment affecting different areas of your life (finances, friendships, marriage, parenting, etc.)?

Spend some time continuing to draw the Eph 1.

4: ALL THREE

One man I spent time with had been saved for years. He loved Jesus. He went to seminary and shared Jesus regularly. However, he rarely had consistent intimacy with God. We walked through his relationship individually with the Father, Son, and Holy Spirit. We discovered he had little relationship with the Father and even less with the Spirit. His difficulty with the Father came from his relationship with his earthly father. His difficulty with the Spirit came from a combination of his seminary training and his profession.

He went to a seminary that emphasized exegetical work in the Scriptures but neglected the Holy Spirit. In his professional field, the physical meant everything and the spiritual did not exist. Once the sources of his imbalance were identified, he repented of his sins, forgave his father, and renounced the false teaching he had believed. His relationship with the Father and the Spirit began to grow. Today he walks in life in ways he could not have before.

Another man was strong in the Spirit but not as much in the Son or the Father. Consequently he wrestled with grace and identifying himself as a son of God. He was focused on signs and wonders and became judgmental of Christians who did not experience any.

Many times in Jesus' life He dealt with demon-possessed people in scenes we would love to have seen. Every time, without raising a finger, Jesus forced the demons to leave the people they were terrorizing. On one occasion His power source was challenged. Some people actually accused Him of casting out demons by satanic power. Jesus corrected them by saying, "I cast out demons by the Spirit of God" (Matthew 12:28). His power source was the Holy Spirit. Furthermore, Luke 4:1 says Jesus was, "full of the Holy Spirit." The Holy Spirit was not called on remotely or partially involved in Jesus' life. Jesus lived in intimate relationship with the Holy Spirit who empowered His life.[1]

What about Jesus and His Father? Scripture says Jesus had a deep relationship with His Father. He regularly withdrew from His work to rest in the presence of His Father and pray. He followed His Father's leading, seeking to glorify Him in all things: "I glorified You on the earth, having accomplished the work which You have given Me to do" (John 17:4). He was so intimate with His Father that He could say in John 5:19–20,

Truly, truly, I say to you, the Son can do nothing of Himself, unless it is something He sees the Father doing; for whatever the Father does, these things the Son also does in like manner. For the Father loves the Son, and shows Him all things that He Himself is doing; and the Father will show Him greater works than these, so that you will marvel.

While on earth, Jesus the Son of God lived full of the Holy Spirit in perfect relationship with God the Father.

Jesus' Kingdom way, His Way of Rest, is Trinitarian living. To walk in Jesus' way is to walk in healthy, full relationships with the Father, Son, and Holy Spirit. Consider this: Jesus came not

THE WAY OF REST:

One God: Father, Son, and Holy Spirit

Two Kingdoms

Three Enemies

Four Promises

Five Disciplines

just to forgive you of your sins but to forgive your sins so that you would be reconnected with the Father, Son, and Holy Spirit. "For Christ also died for sins once for all, the just for the unjust, so that He might bring us to God" (1 Peter 3:18). It is amazing to believe and meditate on the truth that God the Father, Son, and Holy Spirit equally love you with perfect love!

This is what it means to walk in Trinitarian balance. Trinitarian balance happens when any person lives in a healthy relationship with the Father, the Son, and the Holy Spirit. Unfortunately, most Christians have some kind of imbalance. They have greater intimacy with one or two persons of the Trinity to the neglect of the other(s). They are strong in the Holy Spirit but weak in Jesus and/or the Father. They have intimacy with the Father and the Son but are hesitant in the Spirit. As we will see, Trinitarian imbalance has profound effects on a person's ability to walk in the promises of God for his or her life. It is not unusual for people to experience great movements of freedom by working through their imbalance. This chapter focuses on Jesus' Trinitarian teachings.

As an aside, one thing you will begin to notice as you open up to Trinitarian balance is how specific the biblical authors were in ascribing particular works to specific persons of the Trinity. The Apostle Paul loved to talk about the different persons of the Trinity. For example, he writes in 2 Corinthians 13:14, "The grace of the Lord Jesus Christ, and the love of God (the Father), and the fellowship of the Holy Spirit, be with you all." He writes in Romans 8:2, "Therefore, there is now no condemnation for those who are in Christ Jesus. For the law of the Spirit of life in Christ Jesus has set you free from the law of sin and of death."[2] Trinitarian balance was what Jesus walked in, and it's what His disciples taught!

THE TRINITY DEFINED

God has always revealed Himself as a Triune God. The people of God have traditionally defined the Trinity in this way:

1. There is only one God.
2. God exists in three distinct persons.
3. Each person is fully God.

This is the orthodox definition of God as He has revealed Himself in Scripture. In Trinitarian balance we amend the definition to include truths about the relationship and roles in the Trinity taught from Jesus and others in the Bible. Relational Trinitarianism is defined as:

1. There is only one God.

2. God exists in three distinct persons in love with each other.

3. Each person is fully God.

4. Each person has distinct responsibilities that the others will not do.

5. We are invited into a loving relationship with the Father, the Son, and the Holy Spirit.

The classic definition has three concepts, whereas the relational definition has five. Let's work through each concept being careful to clearly understand each.

THERE IS ONLY ONE GOD.

Jesus was a monotheist. He believed in one God. He prayed to one God (John 17:1–3), sought one God (John 5:19–20), taught one God (Matthew 22:34–40), and followed one God (Luke 22:39–46).[3]

He had no doubt about the existence of one supernatural, spiritual being who existed before creation, created time, and guided everything according to His holy will. Against polytheism (the worship of many gods), idolatry (worshipping anyone or anything more than God), agnosticism (a belief in some form of spirituality but uncertain on absolute truth), and atheism (rejecting the existence of any god), Jesus believed in one God and enjoyed deep, personal fellowship Him.

GOD EXISTS IN THREE PERSONS WHO ARE IN LOVE WITH EACH OTHER.

This aspect of God is peculiar to the God of the Bible. No other gods reveal themselves to be one God who exists in three distinct persons. The math simply does not add up. Nevertheless, Jesus and the rest of Scripture teach that God exists as three distinct persons who are in perfect love with each other.

In Matthew 28:19, Jesus gives His disciples a command known as the Great Commission: "Go, therefore, and make disciples of all nations, baptizing them in the name of the Father, Son, and Holy Spirit." According to Jesus, the Father, Son, and Holy Spirit are distinct persons equal to each other.[4]

The Apostle Paul teaches in Galatians 4:1–7 that anyone who gives their life to God is adopted into God's family. He says in verse 6, "Because you are sons, God (Father) has sent forth the Spirit of His Son into our hearts, crying, 'Abba! Father!'"[5] The Father, Son, and Holy Spirit are shown to be distinct persons working together to bring reconciliation to man. No matter how unimaginable it may seem to man, God is one God who is three distinct persons. In some regard this should give us comfort and make sense—there should be things about the God of All Creation we just do not understand!

Scripture then teaches us that the Father, Son, and Holy Spirit love each other. They wholly, purely, and perfectly love each other. 1 John 4:8 says, "The one who does not love does not know God, for God is love." In 1 John 4:18, the apostle writes, "There is no fear in love." There is no jealousy, tension, anxiety, doubt, deception, anger, compromise, scheming, pride, or boastfulness among the Father, Son, and Holy Spirit. None. They are deeply, perfectly in love with each other.

EACH PERSON IS FULLY GOD.

In John 8, Jesus claimed to be God Himself. A group of religious leaders called the Pharisees got into a discussion with Him about what it meant to be free. The Pharisees argued that they were related to Abraham, the patriarch of all Israel and the receiver of God's promises; therefore, they were free. Jesus trumped their reliance on their lineage in 8:58 by saying, "Truly, truly I say to you, before Abraham was born, I am."

This may not sound like much to you, but the Jews knew exactly what Jesus was saying. Verse 59 says the Pharisees picked up rocks to stone Him for blasphemy. Jesus had just claimed to be God. "I am" was the name God shared with Moses in Exodus 3. In Exodus, God told Moses to lead the nation of Israel out of Egypt. Moses asked God whom he should say sent him when he goes to lead Israel. God responded, "Thus you shall say to the sons of Israel, 'I AM has sent me to you'" (Exodus 3:14). Jesus claimed to be God, and the Israelites knew it.

Furthermore, the Father is also God. In fact, the Father is regularly called God. In Matthew 6:25–33, Jesus uses Father and God interchangeably. Paul writes in Ephesians 1:2, "Grace to you and peace from God our Father and the Lord Jesus Christ." That the Father is God is widely attested to throughout Scripture.

Finally, we are taught that the Spirit is God. That Jesus names the Spirit alongside the Father and the Son in His Great Commission places the Spirit on equal footing with the Father and the Son. And Jesus says in Mark 3:28–29, "Truly I say to you, all sins shall be forgiven the sons of men, and whatever blasphemies they utter; but whoever blasphemes against the Holy Spirit never has forgiveness, but is guilty of an eternal sin." It is only possible to blaspheme against the Holy Spirit because the Holy Spirit is God.

Many different groups of people and religions deny various aspects of the Trinity. Islam claims the same God but rejects that Jesus is equally God, reducing Him to a prophet. Mormonism and Jehovah's Witnesses also reject the truth that Jesus is God in the flesh. Others have different views on the reality and nature of the Holy Spirit. In spite of these beliefs, God reveals Himself in Scripture as one God who exists as three distinct persons, each fully God, and each in perfect love with one another. Jesus' Kingdom way is Trinitarian, a dynamic, intimate, constant interaction between all three persons.

EACH PERSON HAS RESPONSIBILITIES THE OTHER PERSONS WILL NOT DO.

This is critical to understand for anyone who wants to walk in the way of Jesus. Each person of the Trinity has different responsibilities in creation. The Father has work the Son and Spirit don't have and will not do. The Spirit has work the Father and Son don't have and will not do. The Son has work the Spirit and Father don't have and will not do. This is beautiful because it helps us know and experience the love of all three. And it can help explain why, even though we may love Jesus, we do not experience His life.

The night before Jesus was crucified, He spent time in the Garden of Gethsemane praying. He was in agony while pushing against God's plan for His life. Luke 22:42 records Jesus saying, "Father, if You are willing, remove this cup from Me; yet not My will, but Yours be done." Jesus lived according to the will of His Father. The Father had the plan, not the Son. In fact, Jesus teaches us to pray, "Our Father, who is in heaven, Hallowed be Your name. Your Kingdom come. Your will be done." The Father has the plan—not the Son or the Spirit. Therefore, we should appeal to the Father to make His will known to us.

Galatians 4:1–7 is another great example of Trinitarian responsibilities. The Father sends the Son to redeem us so that we may be adopted, and the Father sends the Spirit into the hearts of those who surrender to Him to seal their adoption. The Son did not send the Father. The Spirit did not redeem us. The Father does not enter our hearts.

Paul clearly details that adoption is the plan of our Father, made possible through the sacrificial death of the Son, and applied to us by the Spirit. Each has a distinct role to perfectly carry out! As God moved man to write Scripture, He was careful to clarify which person of the Trinity was at work. As disciples of Jesus, we want to understand who is responsible for what in our lives.[6]

THE FATHER'S RESPONSIBILITIES

God the Father is the perfection of fatherhood.

- He has a will in creation and for our lives.
  (Matthew 6:9–13 [specifically verse 10b], Romans 12:1–2, Hebrews 10:1–10, Colossians 1:9, 1 John 5:14)
- The Father adopts us into His family, giving us a new identity, and is faithful in providing for all of our needs.
  (Galatians 4:1–7, Matthew 6:9–13 [specifically verse 9]).
- The Father also sets the timing for salvation.
  (Acts 1:6–8, Galatians 4:1–7).

These responsibilities belong exclusively to the Father. If we have a strained relationship with the Father, then we will not enjoy His presence or the benefit of His work.

THE SON'S RESPONSIBILITIES

The Son also has responsibilities in creation and in our lives:

- The Son became incarnate as Jesus. (John 1:1–18, Hebrews 1:1–4)
- The Son offers atonements through his sacrifices. (Romans 10:13, Hebrews 10:10, 14)
- The Son also loves (John 15:9) and gives authority in His name. (Luke 10:1–24, Matthew 28:18–20, Ephesians 2:1–10)

These responsibilities belong exclusively to the Son. If we deny or limit our relationship with Him, then we will not know these truths for our lives.

THE SPIRIT'S RESPONSIBILITIES

The Spirit has many responsibilities as well:

- The Spirit reveals the Father and His will to us.
  (1 Corinthians 2:6–13, Ephesians 1:15–17, Colossians 1:9)
- The Spirit is actively at work in the world and in our lives today.
  (John 14:16–17, 16:5–11, Acts 1:7–8, Ephesians 1:13)
- The Spirit renews and sanctifies us .
  (John 3:3, 1 Corinthians 5:17, Galatians 5:22–23)
- The Spirit empowers us for holiness (Romans 8:1–17) and empowers us for ministry.
  (Luke 4:16–19, Acts 1:7–8, Ephesians 3:14–19)
- The Spirit gifts us (1 Corinthians 12), reveals Jesus (John 15:26–27), gives us intimacy with the Father and the Son (John 14:16, Romans 8:9), and clarifies truth.
  (John 14:26, John 16:12–14)

The Holy Spirit is the One today who conveys the will and love of the Father, the effective work and authority of Jesus, and empowerment for life and ministry. He is fully God. Having a relationship with Him is critical. This is why the New Testament says we can grieve the Holy Spirit, but it does not say we can grieve the Father and the Son. These responsibilities belong exclusively to the Spirit. If we limit the Spirit, then we limit His presence and His effectiveness in our lives.

I hope you are seeing with greater clarity that Jesus lived in healthy relationships with the Father, Son, and Holy Spirit. To walk in Jesus' way is to walk in intimacy with each person of the Trinity.

I discipled a man who struggled with insecurity. He had been in the church a long time and served the Lord by leading worship in small groups. However, he never felt victory or power in his life. We walked through Trinitarian balance and discovered he had difficulties with the Holy Spirit. His difficulties came from experiences with friends while growing up.

A charismatic movement came through his town and many of his friends got involved. This man watched his friends begin to abuse others based on their spiritual experiences. His experience made him very resistant to the Holy Spirit. Consequently, he suffered in his faith. Once we identified the lies he believed, he was freed to enjoy the Spirit and his insecurity faded.

WE ARE INVITED INTO A LOVING RELATIONSHIP WITH THE FATHER, SON, AND HOLY SPIRIT.

We briefly covered this at the beginning of this chapter, but it needs further discussion. When a person comes to faith in Jesus, they're brought from death to life, from the dominion of darkness into the Kingdom of God, and from Satan to the family of God. **We are adopted into Trinitarian, perfect love.** The Father, Son, and Holy Spirit equally, passionately love us.

Let's look again at what Paul writes in 2 Corinthians 13:14. "The grace of the Lord Jesus Christ, and the love of God, and the fellowship of the Holy Spirit, be with you all." Draw deeply into the Trinitarian intimacy of that verse! From the middle of a prayer Jesus makes to His Father in John 17:22–23, Jesus says,

> The glory which You have given Me I have given to them, that they may be one, just as We are one; *I in them* and You in Me, that they may be perfected in unity, so that the world may know that You sent Me, and *loved them, even as You have loved Me* (emphasis added).

Scripture continually adds to the love of each of the Father, Son, and Holy Spirit for the people of God. This is the joy of salvation! We're not just forgiven—we're birthed into perfect, holy, pure, gracious, merciful, Trinitarian love! Part of the glory of the love of the Father, Son, and Holy Spirit is their work to meet us wherever we are, healing and freeing us as we will allow them to work. No matter what the condition of our imbalance may be, God is actively working to restore us.

OTHER TYPES OF IMBALANCE

Trinitarian imbalance can also be caused by putting other persons or things above one, two, or all three persons of the Trinity. Some may place the church, or their role in it, at a level equal to or above God. When God says that we will have no other gods or idols, the church is certainly included (Revelation 2:1–7). Some may elevate the Bible above the Trinity. Jesus warns against this in John 5:38–40. Others may elevate their denominational affiliation higher than God. There may be additional causes not listed that keep a person from intimacy with the Father, Son, and Holy Spirit. As you evaluate your Trinitarian condition, be open to considering other persons or things that you have allowed to have priority over the Father, Son, and Holy Spirit.

HEALING AND RESTORATION

How does a person walking in imbalance find restoration?

The Holy Spirit may lead you to balance on your own. He may lead you to someone who can help you because the issues are so personal you cannot see them. Regardless, restoration begins when the sources of imbalance are identified.

Is the imbalance caused by a bad relationship with an earthly father? Is it caused by a bad experience with a charismatic movement? Is the condition the result of denominational teaching? Is it the result of some traumatic experience? Once the sources of imbalance are identified, a person can respond according to the need.

For example:

- Someone has neglected the Father and his or her family background caused their imbalance. The person was victimized by another family member, but blames their father for not protecting them. The person transferred that anger from their earthly father to God the Father. Restoration happens as the person asks for and receives forgiveness from God the Father. Restoration continues as the person, now full of the love of the Father, Son, and Holy Spirit, forgives his or her earthly father.

- One person is strong in the Holy Spirit but resists Jesus and the Father. It's later discovered that this was caused by a traumatic experience while attending an institutional church. The person equates the Father and the Son with institutionalism. There's an opportunity for the person to ask the Father and the Son for forgiveness, breaking the lie they've believed for years. Once this happens, the person is immediately restored in their relationships with the Father and the Son.

As I discipled a man, he said, "I'm good with God, the Son, and the Spirit." I noticed, however, that every time he referenced the Father, he said, "God." I pointed this out to him.

"I noticed that every time you refer to the Father you say God. How is your relationship with your dad?"

"Terrible."

His relationship with his earthly father was hindering him from even calling God, "Father." He never noticed it because he was in relationship with God. Eventually we worked through his dad issue and were able to enjoy His Father and his identity as son.

Trinitarian imbalance comes in many different forms. Hopefully, through the examples given, anyone will be able to know the path of restoration.

TRINITARIAN PRAYING

In light of the Trinity, prayer can become confusing. To whom are we to pray to? Is it okay to pray to all three?

In the Lord's Prayer, Jesus teaches us to pray to the Father. He begins the prayer by saying, "Our Father who is in heaven" (Matthew 6:9). So Jesus' prayer is addressed to our Father.

Paul offers some great Trinitarian insight in two places that can guide our prayers. First, he writes in Ephesians 2:18, "For through Him (Christ) we both have access in one Spirit to the Father." This passage indicates that we pray by the Spirit and in the Spirit. We pray to the Father by accessing Him through Jesus the Son.

Second, Paul gives a prayer in Ephesians 3:14–21 that provides another example of the specific works of each person in the Trinity:

> For this reason I bow my knees before the Father, from whom every family in heaven and on earth derives its name, that He would grant you, according to the riches of His glory, to be strengthened with power through His Spirit in the inner man, so that Christ may dwell in your hearts through faith; and that you, being rooted and grounded in love, may be able to comprehend with all the saints what is the breadth and length and height and depth, and to know the love of Christ which surpasses knowledge, that you may be filled up to all the fullness of God. Now to Him who is able to do far more abundantly beyond all that we ask or think, according to the power that works within us, to Him be the glory in the church and in Christ Jesus to all generations forever and ever. Amen.

From Jesus and Paul we can conclude that we are to pray to the Father, through Jesus, in the Spirit. However, the Father, Son, and Holy Spirit are all equally God. Therefore, praying to Jesus and the Spirit is certainly not wrong. As we get healthier in Trinitarian balance, our comfort, freedom, and joy in Trinitarian praying will increase.

Do not get discouraged if this feels awkward at first. You walk by grace. The Father, Son, and Holy Spirit love you. Enjoy praying and learning to pray!

CONCLUSION

Jesus' way of life is Trinitarian living. It's exciting to consider the reality that you are loved fully and equally by the Father, Son, and Holy Spirit. It's wonderful to walk in intimacy with each, knowing Them and being known by Them. Imbalance is a crippling condition that is the cause of so many issues in a person's life. It's unfortunate how pervasive such imbalance is.

ALL THREE: CHAPTER WORK

Begin your time reflecting on each person of the Trinity. As you move from one to another, consider how much each loves each other and each loves you. Write anything you see or feel here.

1. Read Titus 3:3–7, Romans 5:1–5, and John 14:26. Note the Trinitarian activity in each.

2. With which person(s) of the Trinity do you have the most intimacy?

3. With which person(s) of the Trinity do you have the least intimacy?

4. Make a column for each person of the Trinity with whom you do not have great intimacy. Write the person's name at the top of the column. Underneath each column, write the issues that keep you from deeper intimacy. After writing your initial list, ask the Holy Spirit to reveal other issues you may have that you're not aware of.

5. Respond to each issue by asking for forgiveness for allowing that specific issue to keep you from intimacy. After you ask for forgiveness, receive it! Many people continually ask for forgiveness that has already been given—they have just not received it. Embrace the new condition of your relationship! As you continue to seek God in His Word, enjoy the ways the different authors write about the persons of the Trinity.

5: FAKE DUCKS AND REAL WAR

I cannot say this emphatically enough: **JESUS LIVED AT WAR!** While reading about His life, you're thrust onto the front lines of a soldier engaged in daily combat. Bombs drop and bullets fly. Jesus' Kingdom way, the Way of Rest, is lived in the midst of a universal, cosmological, spiritual, internal war—and casualties are everywhere.

Battle-training is a required part of the curriculum for anyone who wants to take Jesus' yoke upon themselves and learn from Him. He had rest, not because there was no war, but because He knew how to fight.

I had a roommate, Rob, who loved to hunt ducks. Dressed in the most appropriate camouflage for the day, he would leave the house at 4:00 a.m. to get to his spot before the ducks would fly overhead. He took a huge net of decoys and a duck call or whistle. When he got to his spot, he would set his decoys in the best places and then hide. At the right time, he would blow his duck call to lure ducks close enough to shoot them. The ducks were unaware that they were flying into a war. They were unaware that an enemy lurked, seeking to deceive them into believing they could have safe landings. They were unaware that the ducks they saw were actually wood masquerading as real ducks. Nevertheless, the ducks were at war.

When Rob didn't kill any ducks, he was disappointed. After unsuccessful trips, he would work on perfecting his duck call, or buy better decoys or more appropriate camouflage, and then go out and hunt again. With fake birdcalls and decoys, Rob lured ducks to their deaths. When he wasn't successful, he found new ways to lure and kill. He was determined to become better at deception. In his hunting, Rob used every means he could to kill ducks.

Another way to say this is that *Rob used fake ducks to make real ducks dead ducks.*

This illustrates the reality and severity of the war in which we live. 1 John 5:19 says, "We know that we are of God, and that the whole world lies in the power of the evil one." Jesus taught that the Holy Spirit was going to come and convict the world concerning judgment "because the ruler of this world has been judged" (John 16:11).

THE WAY OF REST:

One God

Two Kingdoms: God vs. Satan

Three Enemies

Four Promises

Five Disciplines

Paul wrote in Ephesians 6:12, "For our struggle is not against flesh and blood, but against the rulers, against the powers, against the world forces of this darkness, against the spiritual forces of wickedness in the heavenly places." With many other passages we are taught that we're born into a war between **two kingdoms**. The Kingdom of God is firmly set against the dominion of Satan. Colossians 1:13–14 says, "For He rescued us from the domain of darkness, and transferred us to the Kingdom of His beloved Son, in whom we have redemption, the forgiveness of sins."

From the time of Adam and Eve's fall in the Garden of Eden to Jesus' return in Revelation, war is the context and condition of life. In the Old Testament the war between the kingdoms is seen mainly in the battles between God's people, Israel, and its surrounding countries. These are a shadow of the greater war in the spiritual realm. In the Gospels, the spiritual reality of the war becomes more prevalent as Jesus engages in battles against demonic forces.

The connection between the spiritual and physical forces in both kingdoms is easier to see. In the remainder of the New Testament, the disciples of Jesus continue to fight in the war, training us to do the same. The Bible ends in the book of Revelation with the details of how the final battle will be fought. The reality of the war helps explain so much of our life experience. War is cold. The enemies of Jesus and His people do not care. They do not fight fair. They are not just. They are calculating, deceptive, expert killers.

- "The thief comes only to steal and kill and destroy" (John 10:10a).

- "For such men are apostles, deceitful workers, disguising themselves as apostles of Christ. No wonder, for even Satan disguises himself as an angel of light" (2 Corinthians 11:13–15).

- "Submit therefore to God, resist the devil and he will flee from you" (James 4:7).

- "Be of sober spirit, be on the alert. Your adversary, the devil, prowls around like a roaring lion, seeking someone to devour" (2 Peter 5:8).

These verses do not describe some vague notion called evil. They describe an enemy of God and the people of God who are actively and intently at work to destroy life.

We have to learn how to fight from Jesus. Not training to fight is like teaching children to ride bikes but not teaching them about traffic! So many brothers and sisters suffer unnecessarily because they're unaware of the war. Like the ducks, they have not been awakened to the enemy, his tactics, and the availability of freedom. Nevertheless, the war rages. Casualties mount. Let us lean into Jesus, the Light of the world, and let Him train our hands for battle!

As for God, His way is blameless;
The word of the Lord is tried;
He is a shield to all who take refuge in Him.
For who is God, but the Lord?
And who is a rock, except our God,
The God who girds me with strength
And makes my way blameless?
He makes my feet like hinds' feet,
And sets me upon my high places.
He trains my hands for battle,
So that my arms can bend a bow of bronze.
You have also given me the shield of Your salvation,

And Your right hand upholds me;

And Your gentleness makes me great.

You enlarge my steps under me,

And my feet have not slipped (Psalm 18:30–36).

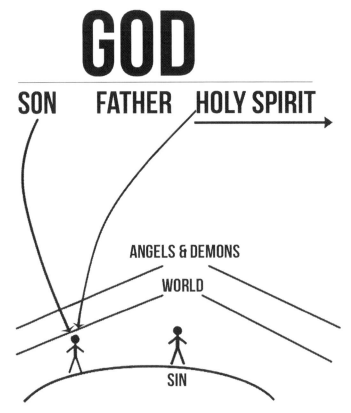

The reality of the war as seen in the Eph 1 diagram.

THE HISTORY OF THIS WAR

Using the duck-hunter analogy, where did the duck hunter come from? Why is he here? How does he work? Why are we so prone to follow his call? Are there other forces at work? How did we get where we are?

"In the beginning God created the Heavens and the Earth" (Genesis 1:1) On the sixth day He created man and woman in His image and after His likeness. They were the unique image-bearers of God. After He completed His sixth day of work, God saw all that He made and it was very good. Everything was as God intended. There was no sin, no sickness, and no injustice. There was God the Father, Son, and Holy Spirit, the angels, man and woman, and the Garden of Eden.

In that divine perfection, God gave man a mandate. First, He said, "Be fruitful and multiply, and fill the earth, and subdue it" (Genesis 1:28). Second, He said, "From any tree of the garden you may eat freely; but from the tree of the knowledge of good and evil you shall not eat, for in the day that you eat from it you will surely die" (Genesis 2:16–17). Our Father gave Adam and Eve the perfection of the garden to enjoy. He created them to be His people and for Him to be their God. That relationship was to be built on love, trust, and obedience.

One of many questions about the garden is why would God even put the tree of the knowledge of good and evil there? Why not just leave it out? Then there is no temptation, no fall, and no need for Jesus. Why put it there? The answer comes from the nature of love. God made man to be in a love relationship with Him. How was man to demonstrate his love for God?

God the Father, Son, and Holy Spirit are perfect. Their love comes from the nature of their perfection. However, man is not God. There had to be a way, something, for man to show his love for God. God gave them the tree. The tree gave Adam and Eve a way to demonstrate their love for God by trusting Him and obeying His words regarding the tree. Their love would be demonstrated through obedience.

Jesus regularly teaches us that obedience is the natural product of love. He says in John 14:15 "If you love Me, you will keep My commandments." And again in John 14:21, "He who has My commandments and keeps them is the one who loves Me; and he who loves Me will be loved by My Father, and I will love him and will disclose Myself to him." And finally in John 15:10, Jesus says again, "If you keep My commandments, you will abide in My love; just as I have kept My Father's commandments and abide in His love." Obedience is the mark of love.

Notice in John 15:10 that Jesus' own love for His Father is demonstrated by His obedience. Jesus, who lived a perfect life, enjoyed obedience. We will get into our disdain for obedience later in this section.

God did not put the tree of the knowledge of good and evil in the garden to tempt Adam and Eve, but to give them an opportunity to show their love for God. He was their God and they were going to live life trusting Him with their lives.

So there's God's perfection: angels, man and woman, and the Garden. However, when we get to Genesis 3:1, something has gone terribly wrong. We're introduced to a mysterious "serpent" that's more crafty than all of the animals. Of course, this is Satan who has come to usurp God's plan for His image-bearers. But where did he come from and what authority does he have today?

From Isaiah 14:3–23 and Ezekiel 28:1–19, we gain some insight into what happened. When I share the background of this war, I may refer to the Scripture passages, or I may just tell the story. Circumstances in the conversation determine the course of action.

According to these passages, Satan was once an angel named Lucifer. He became jealous of the glory of God and wanted more for himself. He rebelled against God. God judged his rebellion and kicked him out of the Divine Assembly. (Divine Assembly is another way of saying free access to the regular presence of the Father, Son, and Holy Spirit.) Somehow, and we are not told how, Satan convinced one-third of the angels to follow him in rebellion against God. From this treason the demonic army began.

What began in the heavens came to earth. Satan went after the object of God's affection: man. Satan tempted Eve to rebel against God and His word for their lives. Adam did not stand against his wife's disobedience but joined her, and man was now guilty of the same rebellion. It's worth noting that Satan attacked Eve in the place of her image. Satan challenged how she saw herself, how God saw her, and how she saw God. Through curiosity about becoming something more, she was lured into dissatisfaction with the image that God had created her in. She was deceived into believing that God's restriction was constricting her life, when in fact God's restriction promoted life.

Nevertheless, God came and judged the serpent, the woman, and the man. In Genesis 3:14–19, God doles out the consequences. As a result of the Genesis 3 events, there are now **three enemies at work in creation: Satan, the world, and sin**.[7] Each actively and aggressively wars against God, His will, and His people.

THE WAY OF REST:

One God

Two Kingdoms

Three Enemies: Sin, the World, and Satan

Four Promises

Five Disciplines

This is a brief summation of how we got where we are in life today. Now we're going to look at each enemy individually.

SATAN

The duck hunter considers every detail in his preparation for the hunt. He will choose appropriate clothing, the right location, and the best time. He will spend hours learning to make the best-sounding duck call he can make. He will put out the choicest of decoys. He knows the game in duck hunting is *deception*. He labors to be a master deceiver. If the real ducks get any sense of the hunter, they will not come near.

Satan is a master hunter. He's been at it a long time. It's always sobering for me to consider that somehow Satan convinced a third of the angels to leave the manifest presence of God. The degree of deception he had to have used is tough to describe. That is the effectiveness of his work. He is intense, extremely subtle, and works in toeholds. He will use Scripture, pain, dreams, religion, love, pride, food, drugs, sex and anything else he can to succeed. He is real.

He is alive. He is working. And he is devouring people. This is no game. It is not cute. He does not fight fair. This is real and destructive. He is masterful at deceiving people from the love, grace, and truth of the Father, Son, and Holy Spirit.

So how can one know when Satan is at work in their lives?[8] There are at least seven ways to determine when Satan is attacking. The primary way is through the Holy Spirit. As you are walking in Him, He will show you an area of your life where the enemy is attacking. The role of the Holy Spirit is to guide you into all truth. Part of that truth includes alerting you to deception.

More often, however, the Holy Spirit will work through one of these remaining ways. A second way is by knowing Satan's intent. No matter what his specific attack looks like, Satan always wants to do two things: take glory from God and separate His people from Him. Job 1-3 describes a scene where God, Satan, and Job are the main participants. Satan claims that the only reason Job is faithful to God and intimate with Him is because God has protected Job. God gives Satan permission to attack Job. Satan's goal is to separate Job from God by getting Job angry at God because of trials he must endure.

In the Garden of Eden, Satan tempts Adam and Eve to sin. The effect of their sin is separation from God. They moved from a place of faithfully trusting God to a place of hiding in shame and guilt. When we understand that Satan always works to rob God of His glory and separate His people from His love, seeing satanic attacks becomes easier. If a person feels like no one cares, no one will listen, and no one can understand what they're going through, then it is more than likely that Satan is at work.

A third way to determine Satan's involvement is by knowing his names. The names of Satan reveal his character and his tactics. In Scripture he is called:

- *Satan* (Matthew 4:10, Job 1:6). This name means adversary. Satan works against God's will in people's lives. He may use fear, discouragement, distraction or a number of other weapons. Here he stands opposed to the direction of God for His people's lives.

- *Devil* (Matthew 4:1, 13:39; Revelation 12:9). This name means slanderer or false accuser. Satan works to call people names, remind them of things past, and confuse them about the faithfulness of God.

- *Serpent* (Genesis 3:1, 14; 2 Corinthians 11:3). This name is used to highlight Satan's deceptive nature. He can take different forms and speak through different people. He does not just come straight forward or through one person.

- *Be-elzebul, Ruler of this world, Prince of the power of the air* (Matthew 10:25, 12:24; Luke 11:15, John 12:31, Ephesians 2:2). Be-elzebul means lord of the house. All three names have the same connotation. Satan is lord over the world. He exercises his authority from what Paul calls the air. We will see in the next section how Satan uses his authority. But it is important to understand he does have real authority.

- *Evil one* (Matthew 13:19, 1 John 2:13). It's pretty clear what this means. But here we pick up the nature of his intent. The being of Satan is evil. His works are evil. Evil is the enemy of God's goodness. Satan's intent is to bring desolation, destruction, and division.

- *Father of lies* (John 8:44). This is clear as well. He is the master liar. If he cannot get in with one lie he will get in with another. And if neither works he will lay in wait until an opportune time to return.

- *The Tempter* (Genesis 3:1–3, Luke 4:1-13, Matthew 16:23). Satan works through tempting. He lies, tempting people to question what they believe or to never pursue truth at all. Notice that in the wilderness with Jesus, Satan tried three different ways to tempt Him. Like lying, Satan tried to get in one way and it didn't work, so he tried two others. When those failed he waited again until that opportune time.

Understanding these names will help us identify where Satan is working in a person's life. The longer you fight in the war the more apparent Satan and his schemes will be. While he is a master liar, there is only so much he can do.

In addition to his names, knowing Satan's past works helps to determine his present attacks. Scripture shows us many different works of Satan in peoples' lives:

- Stealing the effectiveness of the Word in people's lives (Mark 4:15)
- Physical illness (Luke 13:10–17)
- Possession (Matthew 8:28, Mark 1:32, Luke 8:27)
- Blinding people in unbelief (2 Corinthians 2:11)
- False religions (John 8)
- Discord in the body of Christ (1 Corinthians 4:18–20)
- Extreme bodily harm (Luke 8:30)
- Subverting the will of God (Matthew 16:23)
- Keeping believers in bondage (James 4:7)

In all of these, it's critical to see the supernatural causes of suffering. As followers of Jesus walking in the way of Jesus, we must believe in the presence of supernatural causes. Any type of illness can be purely physical. But, according to Jesus, it can also be purely spiritual. Depression can be a result of hormonal imbalance, spiritual attack, or a combination of both.) To not consider demonic causes for the suffering we endure is to miss the war and the teachings of Jesus. A fifth way of determining a satanic attack is by knowing truth—God's word. Satan works to lie, to pervert truth. The more we know truth the easier it will be to hear the lie. Adam and Eve were given God's word in Genesis 2:15–17. Instead of engaging in conversation with Satan in Genesis 3:1–7, they should have used the word to discern the attack and flee!

I have also found it helpful in determining a satanic attack to rule out other solutions. If quoting Scripture, prayer, serving, and other works are not effective, then that is a good indicator of demonic activity. Scripture and prayer are obviously powerful, but if they are not pointed at the root cause then they become ineffective. When Satan attacks, he attacks specifically. If he is attacking in the area of fear, and a person is praying for God's blessings and memorizing Scripture about spiritual gifts, then those activities will do nothing for their condition. If he is attacking and a person seeks a chemical solution or seeks to modify their own behavior, it will not work. Satanic attacks require spiritual warfare solutions. When other solutions do not work, that can be a good indicator that Satan is responsible.

A final method of determining satanic attack is through the counsel of others. Many times we just cannot see what is happening to us. We need the counsel of brothers and sisters who understand the war. At one point in the relationship between Jesus and Peter, Jesus had to point out that Satan was working in Peter's life. (See Matthew 16:21–23.)

From the beginning, Scripture teaches us about the reality of spiritual causes. You cannot walk with Jesus and disavow spiritual causes in life. You will not be able to effectively disciple people unless you are well versed in spiritual warfare. As you minister to people, you must consider spiritual causes as contributors to their conditions. They may be dealing with something emotional or physical, yet the problem may be spiritual. You must be prepared, or at the very least offer a resource that can help. Then you need to be trained in how to deal with it yourself. We will briefly cover this in the freedom section of the next chapter.[9]

WHAT ABOUT SATAN AND CHRISTIANS?

There are many questions and opinions about the effect Satan and demons can have on Christians. One often-used line says that while demons cannot possess, they can oppress Christians. Christians have been sealed by the Holy Spirit and therefore cannot be possessed by demons. What attack they can bring is minimal. I offer this to you based on my understanding of Scripture and my experience working with people. Demons cannot possess Christians, but they can do a lot more than just oppress. A middle ground sometimes called "attachment" is used to explain the more-than-oppression position.

Demons have the ability to exert influence in areas where Christians have not addressed their issues. The demonic have not "taken over" in the classic sense of possession, but they are also not merely on the outside pointing fingers. They might not have total control, but they exercise substantial influence. It doesn't matter how you label it, whether "attachment" or something else, just know that it is real.

POSSESSION   ATTACHMENT   OPPRESSION

One of many places this can be seen in the Bible is James 4:7. Here James writes, "Submit therefore to God. Resist the devil and he will flee from you." This is the normal pattern that Jesus walks in and that is taught by Paul and Peter. Submission to God empowers a person to resist the devil. You cannot resist without first submitting.

What happens then when a Christian has an area of their lives they are unwilling to submit to the Lord? The person has been baptized and is born again. However, they have experienced a trauma in their life that they do not want to revisit, yet that trauma is the source of their fear. The person reads their Bible faithfully, goes to church, serves, and even receives from the Spirit, but they are unwilling to submit this trauma to the Lord.

How are they able to resist the devil? Resistance requires submission. I have seen people who have memorized all sorts of Scripture, have served in many different capacities, have gone to counseling, have used prescription drugs, have given more money, and have done whatever they could to get free of something, and still experience no victory. At the heart of their condition has been a refusal to acknowledge spiritual warfare and deal with their root issues. Once they're aware of demonic causes and bondage then the Spirit works to free them. The change is dramatic and the results are trajectory-changing.

Another example comes from Ephesians 6.[10] Paul charges Christians to be "strong in The Lord and in the strength of His might." So what happens when Christians are weak in the Lord or in a particular area in their lives?

Paul trains his people to take up the shield of faith "with which you will be able to extinguish all the flaming arrows of the evil one." What happens when a Christian does not take the shield up fast enough? The enemy shoots fiery arrows at specific targets.

When a fiery arrow lands it burns and spreads. One can picture a movie scene where archers light their arrows with fire and shoot them over castle walls. The fiery arrows land on hay or wood and the fire quickly spreads, consuming people and everything else it touches. These arrows can be more severe than demonic oppression. One of Satan's demons has found a way in and is causing damage in a Christian. It may be through fear, approval, anger, pride, guilt, shame, or a host of other things. Nevertheless, the source of the issue is demonic.

Satan and his demonic army are actively and effectually at work in the world and in people. Spiritual causes are very real. There is power and authority in the darkness. They are working to rob our Father of His glory and destroy His work in people. Jesus battled Satan and his demonic army throughout His life, death, and resurrection, and He trains us through the Holy Spirit to do the same.

THE WORLD

In addition to Satan, the world is the second enemy in the war. Returning to our duck analogy, the messages of the world are all of the different fake ducks set out by the hunter to deceive and trap. The goal of the hunter is to create the most realistic fake ducks possible. Attention is given to every quality—shape, size, contours, and colors—in an attempt to lure real ducks into the hunter's net. Hence "the world" can be seen in Scripture as any of the following examples:

- "See to it that no one takes you captive through philosophy and empty deception, according to the tradition of men, according to the elementary principles of the world, rather than according to Christ" (Colossians 2:8).

- "Do not love the world or the things in the world. If anyone loves the world, the love of the Father is not in him. For all that is in the world, the lust of the flesh and the lust of the eyes and the boastful pride of life, is not from the Father, but is from the world. The world is passing away, and also its lusts; but the one who does the will of God lives forever" (1 John 2:15–17).

- "For by these He has granted to us His precious and magnificent promises, so that by them you may become partakers of the divine nature, having escaped the corruption that is in the world by lust" (2 Peter 1:4).

- "If the world hates you, you know that it has hated Me before it hated you. If you were of the world, the world would love its own; but because you are not of the world, but I chose you out of the world, because of this the world hates you" (John 15:18–19).

On the one hand God so loved the world that He gave His Son Jesus. On the other hand the world is aggressively against God and His work. It is hard to define "the world" because it is comprehensive and changes according to time, culture, gender, and other factors. So "the world" for a single woman in Nicaragua will have different attributes than a Muslim man in Iran. In the broadest sense, "the world" is the collective systems, philosophies, governments, and religions that deny the truth of the Father, Son, and Holy Spirit.

What are the cultural messages and family history you have believed? For example, we're taught in the United States that "you can do anything you set your mind to." That is a worldly, cultural message. Another cultural message is, "If you do not take care of yourself, no one else is going to." In our culture, women are taught that to be beautiful they need to maintain a certain weight and look a certain way. Men are told that to be successful they must work seventy to eighty hours per week. In general, these are all examples of cultural messages coming from the United States in general.

Worldly messages come in many different ways:

• Gender	• Education	• Race
• Religion	• Age	• Finances
• Shape	• Politics	• Appearance
• Family	• Region	• Country

While the manifestations of the messages of the world will be different, they have some similar features that make them easier to discern.

- They deny that Jesus is the sufficient sacrifice of God for life (Colossians 2:8–15).
- They pull people away from faithfully following the will of God for their lives (1 John 2:15–17).
- They choke out maturity in the believer (Mark 4:1–20).
- They deny that the way of God is the way of life (Romans 12:2).

As the ruler of the world, Satan is actively at work creating, using, and manipulating the messages of the world as part of his arsenal. This does not mean that there is a demon literally in every pornographic magazine, but it does mean that the enemy is behind the porn industry.

What's important to remember is the enemy's subtlety. Some will rail against Harry Potter but have no problem living in their materialism or gluttony. Materialism and gluttony are far more effective weapons today in the United States than Harry Potter. Laziness and entitlement are effective weapons just like pornography. The messages of the world are everywhere. This is why Jesus and the apostles were so forceful in their condemnation of the world. Instead of going after each individual message, they grouped them into one admonition:

Do not love the world or the things in the world. If anyone loves the world, the love of the Father is not in him. For all that is in the world, the lust of the flesh and the lust of the eyes and the boastful pride of life, is not from the Father, but is from the world. The world is passing away, and also its lusts; but the one who does the will of God lives forever (1 John 2:15–17).

The world is a powerful weapon aimed to separate God and His people. Generally speaking, if everyone is believing it or doing it, we better be real careful with it. Jesus came and fought against the lies and deceits of the world. Walking with Jesus requires walking away from the world.

SIN

Why do ducks continually fall prey to the call of the hunter? Why do people continually chase fake ducks? Why isn't there a generational awakening to the lies and deceit of the enemy?

Sin. Sin. Sin.

Sin is everywhere and in everyone. Sin is brutal, raw selfishness. It is self-centered, self- seeking, powerful, and destructive. It is the internal, destabilizing force of *every* person's life. But by far the worst reality of sin is that it separates the sinner from the Father, Son, and Holy Spirit who loves him or her. Made in the image of God, man was created to be in wonderful relationship with God. God's intent was that man would eternally choose to trust Him, be faithful to Him, and enjoy life with Him as the Father, Son, and Spirit do with each other. Man's desire for "more" ripped that apart and still rips it apart today.

While Satan and the world operate outside of man (in general), sin works inside of man. Sin is an internal condition of rebellion against God. Sin is personal. Sin chooses the fake ducks of Satan over the love of God. By choosing to eat of the tree, Adam and Eve disobeyed God. They chose to break relationship with Him. Sin is no victimless crime. Every sin is a choice to rebel against the Father, Son, and Holy Spirit. It is a denial of *His* way of life. It is personal.

Now, Paul gives us wise insight about sin in Galatians 5:16–17. "But I say, walk by the Spirit, and you will not carry out the desire of the flesh. For the flesh sets its desire against the Spirit, and the Spirit against the flesh; for these are in opposition to one another, so that you may not do the things you please." The flesh has power. Paul then writes that the flesh manifests itself in all of the specific sins we battle, so that the specific sin is not really the issue. The greater issue is the flesh, often called the sinful nature, which empowers the sin.[11] Satan is fine with disciples who want to work on a particular sin issue. He knows there is no power in that because it doesn't address the power source.

In the diagram below you can see the power source of the flesh driving different manifestations of sin. Can you now see how the one with fear can relate to the one with pride? The power is all the same. Can you see that simply dealing with fear is a waste of time? How much more powerful to crucify the flesh! When the flesh is crucified then the power of sin is broken. In dealing with the bondage of sin we work in the power of the Spirit to destroy the power of the flesh.

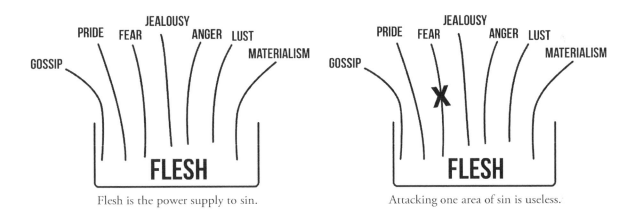

Flesh is the power supply to sin.　　　Attacking one area of sin is useless.

Whether a person's sin was the direct work of the demonic or the world doesn't matter. Every person is responsible for their own sin. Everyone is accountable. One of the great effects of sin is deflection. From the beginning, Adam tried to deflect his responsibility: "The woman whom you gave to be with me, she gave me from the tree, and I ate" (Genesis 3:12).

We all attempt to pass responsibility to others. God our Father will have none of that. We are responsible. We will see that being restored to full and personal responsibility is one of the great places of freedom and joy in life. No one is able to say, "The devil made me do it."

James gives us a vivid description of the process of sin and how it works in us. He writes in James 1:13–15:

> Let no one say when he is tempted, 'I am being tempted by God'; for God cannot be tempted by evil, and He Himself does not tempt anyone. But each one is tempted when he is carried away and enticed by his own lust. Then, when lust has conceived, it gives birth to sin; and when sin is accomplished, it brings forth death.

Do you see the process of sin? We must be careful to not underestimate the power of sin. A man and a woman walk into a room where other women are. The man is tempted to lust while the woman is tempted to judge. The feeling is intense and "feels" debilitating. It seems to come out of nowhere. If they do not know how to identify and combat their temptations, then, as James says, temptation will give birth to sin, which will bring forth death.

Thankfully, Jesus knows the reality and power of sin and equips us in the fight. "For He Himself was tempted in that which He has suffered, He is able to come to the aid of those who are tempted" (Hebrews 2:18). "For we do not have a High Priest (Jesus) who cannot sympathize with our weaknesses, but One who has been tempted in all things as we are, yet without sin" (Hebrews 4:15). Jesus is intimately familiar with the pull of sin and stands as our champion against it.

SOURCES OF SIN

There are four sources of sin in our lives. As you familiarize yourselves with these you will be equipped to deal with them throughout your day.

The first source of sin is **original sin**. Original sin refers to the consequences given to Adam and Eve when they rebelled against God in the Garden of Eden. As a result of their actions, all men and women bear the marks of Adam and Eve's sin. What is remarkable is that original sin manifests itself differently in women and men according to Genesis 3:16–19.

When God cursed Eve, he cursed her in her roles as wife and mother. Therefore, today and all days until Jesus returns, women suffer the sin of Eve in insecurity as wives and mothers. These are two deep places of instability in all women. Consequently, women have a difficult time surrendering these areas of their lives to God and trusting in His provision. Acknowledging that these are areas of vulnerability to sin will position a woman to fight against them and rest in the love and faithfulness of her Father.

Men experience sin in the workplace and in their legacies. These are his greatest places of insecurity. In God's curse on man He says man's work will produce "thorns and thistles." Man will never get out of his work what he puts into it. This creates insecurity in his ability to provide and in his sense of accomplishment. God also says that man will return to dust, "For you are dust, and to dust you shall return" (Genesis 3:19). This is not good for men who want to make a name for themselves and leave a legacy. Understanding that the instability in these areas is sin passed on from Adam equips men to stand against these attacks and live in the way of Christ.

A second source of sin is **generational sin**, which is sin passed from one generation to the next. Like original sin, generational sin is a pre-existing condition. It is something someone is born into. One great example of generational sin is found in the lineage of King David. There's no indication from David's father, Jesse, that sex and idolatry were generational issues. But track how sex entered David's line and was passed to Solomon. See how Solomon added idolatry. Watch how that spread and the damage it did. Generational sin is powerful. You will need to know if what you're dealing with is generational.

A third source of sin is **personal sin**. Personal sins are those we have done all on our own. While we are absolutely responsible for every sin we commit, personal sins describe sin that is not directly connected to original or generational sin. A man who has no family history of anxiety develops an anxiety issue because he cannot trust the Lord with a specific area of his life. This is an example of a sin not directly related to the garden or to generations. These are sins that a person is living in which are not directly caused by the other three areas. From what I have experienced, the most dominant, controlling sins in this area are:

- Alcohol/drugs
- Money
- Sex
- The occult
- Unforgiveness: this is one of the major issues we encounter. Victimization is everywhere. We work to differentiate between being victimized and being a victim.

There are certainly many other areas of sin. Scripture has lists.[12] These are the ones I come across most often in those that I have spent time with.

CONCLUSION

It does not take much time reading the life of Jesus to see that He lived at war. Sin, the world, and Satan have aligned themselves against the love and faithfulness of the Father, Son, and Holy Spirit. Jesus came to fight. He came to win. He came to overcome every enemy of God. And He came to train His disciples to continue His fight in the power of the Holy Spirit. The war is pervasive, affecting every part and person of creation. There are no exceptions. Understanding the brutality of two kingdoms in conflict should give you greater insight into the experiences of your life and those of others. Life at war is completely different than life not at war. This world is broken. To walk in Jesus' Way of Rest is to embrace the reality of war, reject the world, and learn how to stand in the faith.

Thankfully, in His grace and mercy, our Almighty Father faithfully sent His Son to be *the* Light for man. In the midst of the war there is Hope. God *promises* us deliverance and victory in this life. He has not left us. He does not leave us. In the next chapter we will work through the hope of God anchored in His faithfulness and the brilliant sufficiency of Jesus.

FAKE DUCKS AND REAL WAR: CHAPTER WORK

Begin your time reflecting on the reality of war. Consider all that you know about Jesus' life and how often He fought. Bless the Lord for opening your eyes to see the reality of the world that you live in. Write any thoughts and/or feelings you have.

1. How does war help explain various difficulties and experiences in your life, your families' lives, and in the lives of others?

2. How does belief in two kingdoms in conflict and three sources of bondage affect a person's practices?

3. In what ways or in what times have you seen Satan at work in your life? In others' lives?

4. In what ways or in what times have you believed the world's messages?

5. How do you see yourself operating in sin?

      Garden sin:

      Generational:

      Personal:

6. How does it impact you to know that there are three enemies actively seeking to destroy your life and take you away from intimacy with the Father, Son, and Holy Spirit?

Continue to draw out the Eph 1. You should have great wisdom now in the condition of the world as seen in the diagram. Keep at it. You're doing great!

6: RESCUED PART 1

How many times have you heard or read a story where it seems like all hope is lost? The situation is bleak and no one can see any way of victory. Then, just before the enemy brings complete desolation, the hero bursts in and saves the day.

Scripture says that in the fullness of time God sent the Light to pierce the darkness. A beam of Divine Light sliced through the thick shroud of black covering creation. The Son of God came in the flesh. "And the Word became flesh, and dwelt among us, and we saw His glory, glory as of the only begotten from the Father, full of grace and truth" (John 1:14). "In Him was life, and the life was the Light of men. The Light shines in the darkness, and the darkness did not comprehend it" (John 1:4–5).

Jesus is the hope of the world. He is God's answer to the war. He is the Light that no form of darkness can overcome. He is victory. Death could not hold Him. Satan could not stop Him. Sin could not touch Him. In every way and in all things Jesus won. Paul says, "If Christ has not been raised, your faith is worthless; you are still in your sins. . . . If we have hoped in Christ in this life only, we are of all men most to be pitied" (1 Corinthians 15:17, 19). Every inch of creation and every person created have abundant hope in this life solely because of Jesus.

Jesus came to accomplish four things. First, He came to re-establish the Kingdom of God on Earth. As we've seen, Jesus announced His Kingdom intentions in His first recorded sermon in Mark 1:15. "The time is fulfilled, and the Kingdom of God is at hand; repent and believe in the Gospel." Second, He came to destroy Satan and His works. "The Son of God appeared for this purpose, to destroy the works of the devil" (1 John 3:8). Third, He came to defeat the world. "In the world you have tribulation, but take courage; I have overcome the world." And fourth, Jesus came to pay for sin, reconciling man to God. "In this is love, not that we loved God, but that He loved us and sent His Son to be the propitiation for our sins" (1 John 4:10). Mission accomplished.

GOD IS FAITHFUL

Now, the sending of Jesus was not a last-minute response of the Father. It was not that the war somehow became worse than God expected and He said, "I never thought it would get this bad. I'm sending my Son to fix this." No. Jesus came as a fulfillment of God's promise in Genesis 3. In the Garden of Eden, as He was giving consequences to Satan, Adam, and Eve, God promised that He would send one who could crush the enemy (Genesis 3:14–15). From that time forward, those who followed God looked for the Messiah, the chosen one of God who would win the war. Jesus is Messiah (John 4:25).

The Messiah came because God was faithful to His promise. Throughout Scripture, God constantly demonstrates that He is faithful to all of His promises. When God delivered the people of Israel from their Egyptian slavery, He led them into a desert wilderness they had never been in before. Deuteronomy 8:3 tells us why God did this:

He humbled you and let you be hungry, and fed you with manna which you did not know, nor did your fathers know, that He might make you understand that man does not live by bread alone, but man lives by everything that proceeds out of the mouth of the Lord.

God intentionally put Israel in a position where they would have to learn that He is faithful. The first lesson God wanted to imprint on the DNA of Israel's belief was His faithfulness.

If there is any one secret to the Kingdom way of Jesus, it's that He lived in perfect belief that His Father was faithful. He lived moment-by-moment knowing that there was a supernatural, invisible God who was His Father, who was actively involved in His life, and who took care of Him and led Him. This was the underlying truth that freed Jesus to trust in His Father's will, even in His crucifixion.

Can you imagine what your life would look like if you lived every moment of every day believing that the God of all creation was faithful to you?

The glory of the Gospel of Jesus Christ says that He is! As God was faithful to His Son, so too is He faithful to all of His children. Jesus taught His disciples the secret of His way in Matthew 6:31–33:

> Do not worry then, saying, 'What will we eat?' or 'What will we drink?' or 'What will we wear for clothing?' For the Gentiles eagerly seek all these things; for your heavenly Father knowns that you need all these things. But seek first His kingdom and His righteousness, and all these things will be added to you.

God is faithful to you! As God cared for Jesus He will care for you. There is a supernatural, invisible God who is your Father, who is actively involved in your life, and who will provide for you and lead you. As He was faithful to send Jesus according to a promise He made in Genesis 3, so too has God made His children promises that *He will fulfill*.

Paul writes in 2 Corinthians 1:20, "For as many as are the promises of God, in Him they are yes; therefore also through Him is our Amen to the glory of God through us." When God invites us into a relationship with Him and into His Kingdom, He promises that He will be faithful to us. Look at the significance of God's promises in our lives in 2 Peter 1:2–3:

Grace and peace be multiplied to you in the knowledge of God and of Jesus our Lord; seeing that His divine power has granted to us everything pertaining to life and godliness, through the true knowledge of Him who called us by His glory and excellence. For by these He has *granted us* His precious and magnificent promises, so that by them *you may become* partakers of the divine nature, having escaped the corruption that is *in the world by lust* (emphasis added).

According to Peter, God exercises His power in us, overthrowing the power of sin, the world, and Satan, and gives us everything we need *according to His promises*. He is faithful! If He does not keep his promises, we could not walk in everything pertaining to life and godliness. As we learn to walk in His promises, we partake of and have fellowship with the divine nature. That divine nature is God Himself.

In the Way of Rest, we follow Jesus by actively depending on God and His promises for life. This promised life requires us to trust God. Just as He did for the people of Israel who were in the wilderness, God must daily be in our lives or we're not going to survive. We must believe in His promise that He will take care of us. We know He has taught us to pray, "Give us this day our daily bread." We know from Genesis to Revelation that He has shown Himself to be fantastically dependable. If we're going to experience victory in the war and intimacy with Him, we must learn to trust His word for our lives.

Therefore, in what might be a hopeless situation of war and bondage, we are hope-filled because of the faithfulness of God according to His promises. "May the God of peace fill you with all joy and peace in believing that you may abound in hope by the power of the Holy Spirit" (Romans 15:13). We do not have to fear the war because God has responded by sending Jesus, promising life and eternal life to those who will follow Him. He speaks into the darkness and offers a transformational relationship for those who will trust Him. He shows us that life is absolutely possible today.

For the remainder of this chapter we're going to show that the promises of God are ours by grace alone. We cannot earn them and do not have to perform for them. And we're going to show that God's promises come to us only through the person and work of Jesus Christ.

GOD'S PROMISES COME BY GRACE ALONE

The radical and difficult-to-believe reality of God's promises is that He gives them to us by grace. We do not earn and cannot earn what He has for us. No amount of human effort, personality, talent, technology, knowledge, or money can attain the faithfulness and promises of God. God offers Himself to us by grace alone. Paul writes in Ephesians 2:8–9, "For by grace you have been saved through faith; and that not of yourselves, it is the gift of God; not as a result of works, so that no one may boast." Life in the way of Jesus is not life earned but life received.

Grace is one of the most amazing and confounding realities of walking with Jesus. God's grace has brought many weary and exhausted people to tears. The Holy Spirit has awakened people to grace and the liberation has been fantastic. Grace is one of the beautiful gifts from God that all who walk with Him can enjoy. The following diagram shows us how God graciously brings us into His presence and promises:

This diagram depicts what we affectionately call "Grace Mountain." Grace Mountain contrasts the futility of man's works with the grace of God's love.

We're all born into the Valley of Works. In this valley we're separated from God, left to strive in our own energy to find the acceptance, security, and significance every one of us needs. The points listed in the valley represent different ways a person tries to achieve peace in their lives. These will be different for each person, but everyone has them. In the valley, we live believing that we can, we should, and we ought. Ruled by the tyranny of pride, we believe we have the ability to have a blessed life. We will strive to get it or quit under the strain of failure. Life in the valley is empty, unstable, and deeply disappointing.

In the Old Testament, the entire book of Ecclesiastes is dedicated to describing the futility of man's efforts to earn blessing in life. Whether a person pursues wisdom, riches, work, pleasure, or any other means apart from God, Solomon concludes that everything is "vanity and striving after wind" (Ecclesiastes 2:11). This is life lived in the Valley of Works.

Furthermore, Grace Mountain compares the blessings of God to the "blessings" of man. The difference in heights between the valley and the peak of Grace Mountain is indicative of the surpassing richness of life in the presence of God. Life in the valley pales compared to life in the Lord. Before the Apostle Paul began following Jesus, He excelled in every area of his culture. He was at the top in his heritage, education, religion, stature, and power. He thought it was great. Then he ran into the grace of Jesus.

But whatever things were gain to me, those things I have counted as loss for the sake of Christ. More than that, I count all things to be loss in view of the surpassing value of knowing Christ Jesus my Lord (Philippians 3:7–8).

Valley "blessings" fall flat in light of the glory of walking in the love and faithfulness of God and His grace. The way of Christ is just better.

Grace Mountain also shows us our need for help. Consider that our condition is so depraved that it required the Son of God to come and fix it. He is no small solution. It is not as if you have a headache and just need some medicine. We're so bad that the Son of God had to leave heaven, endure what He did, and be resurrected so that healing could be available. Grace puts a deadly nail in the pride of man! There is no requirement to perform or expectation of perfection. God's grace joyfully shouts, "NO, you cannot! Yes, I CAN." Accepting your NO and embracing God's YES is utmost in experiencing the wonders of grace.

Finally, Grace Mountain shows us that man needs grace alone. God's grace is not mixed with other ways to live in other areas of life. Grace is an all-or-nothing offer. You either live in total grace or no grace. Walking in all the goodness of God in Jesus is to walk away from every other way of living. Paul writes in Romans 12:2, "And do not be conformed any longer to the pattern of this world, but be transformed by the renewing of your mind, so that you may prove what the will of God is, that which is good and acceptable and perfect."

In Colossians 2:20–21, Paul writes, "If you have died with Christ to the elementary principles of the world, why, as if you were living in the world, do you submit yourself to decrees, such as, 'Do not handle, do not taste, do not touch!'" In 1 John 1:5–10, the apostle says that we cannot have the Light and walk in darkness. To walk in grace is to sever relationships with the ways of the world and embrace God and the way of grace. Who we are, what we have, and what we do is no longer earned. Everything we are, have, and do is given by grace.

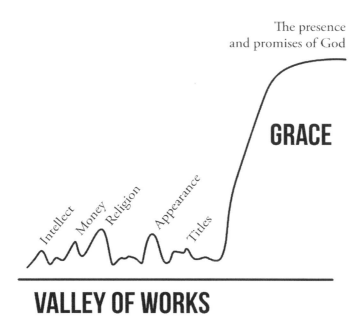

GRACE EFFECTS

When I was in middle school my family lived in Colorado Springs, Colorado. We could see Pikes Peak out of our kitchen window. The peak is 14,110 feet above sea level. At the summit, so many things change just by being there.

You can see for miles. You breathe differently. Your perspective changes. You feel a sense of awe at the height and the expanse. On the right day, you're on top of the clouds! Now, these changes happen just by being on the peak. A person does not have to force themselves to see things differently. These changes occur just by the nature of being on top of the mountain. No one earns the new things. Change happens organically.

Likewise, God's grace changes people.

Even now, as you read these words, you can feel the difference as you awaken to the reality that you're in the presence of God. Breathe deeply. See yourself in presence of God. Look around. Breathe again. What do you see? Who do you see? How do you see yourself? Your problems? Breathe again. Worry, fear, pride, guilt, shame—they all start to fall away. Loneliness is replaced by a profound sense of intimacy. Exhaustion fades. The weight of the world leaves.

How much of this have you earned? This is grace and this is what grace does. Grace transforms people. All of the promises of God and His faithfulness to fulfill them belong to you by grace. Because grace is so rare in our lives—no other religion or philosophy has it—learning to walk in it can be awkward. Like a newborn we must continually receive grace, allowing the Holy Spirit to teach us how to live by it.

THE PROMISES OF GOD COME BY GRACE ALONE IN JESUS ALONE

God can give us His promises by grace alone because of what Jesus Christ has done. The perfect life, ministry, death, and resurrection of Jesus have paid the price for our sin to make the promises of God available to all by grace. If anyone is in Him, they have full access to everything God has. We need nothing else. There are no works. There is no effort. If anyone gives his or her life to Jesus, they are raised up and seated with Christ in the heavenlies. They are given every spiritual blessing. They are made new. They are empowered. They are adopted. They enter into the Kingdom of God.

Jesus has made the way. He has paid the price. He is the one-time sacrifice. No man, or even the collection of all men, can add a drop of anything to what Jesus has done.

Jesus' defeat of sin:

"For if we have become united with Him in the likeness of His death, certainly we shall also be in the likeness of His resurrection, knowing this, that our old self was crucified with Him, in order that our body of sin might be done away with, so that we would no longer be slaves to sin; for he who has died is freed from sin" (Romans 6:5–7).

Jesus' defeat of the world:

"These things I have spoken to you, so that in Me you may have peace. In the world you have tribulation, but take courage; I have overcome the world" (John 16:33).

Jesus' defeat of Satan:

"The one who practices sin is of the devil; for the devil has sinned from the beginning. The Son of God appeared for this purpose, to destroy the works of the devil" (1 John 3:8).

Jesus' access to the Father:

"Jesus said to him, 'I am the way, and the truth, and the life; no one comes to the Father but through Me'" (John 14:6).

Jesus and our sanctification:

"By this will we have been sanctified through the offering of the body of Jesus Christ once for all" (Hebrews 10:10).

Jesus and the temple:

"Therefore, brethren, since we have confidence to enter the holy place by the blood of Jesus, by a new and living way which He inaugurated for us through the veil, that is, His flesh, and since we have a great priest over the house of God, let us draw near with a sincere heart in full assurance of faith, having our hearts sprinkled clean from an evil conscience and our bodies washed with pure water" (Hebrews 10:19–22).

Jesus and our new life:

"But may it never be that I would boast, except in the cross of our Lord Jesus Christ, through which the world has been crucified to me, and I to the world. For neither is circumcision anything, nor uncircumcision, but a new creation" (Galatians 6:14–15).

The biblical witness to the sufficiency of Jesus is overwhelming. The presence and promises of God we receive as we live on Grace Mountain have been made available by Jesus alone. We rest in Him. Because He is raised, we too can be raised. We thank our Father for sending Him, and we thank Him for coming. He is everything to us. Other people may tout scientific studies, other religious leaders, government officials, or popular culture icons. For us, you can pile them together and whomever else you want to add and you will not even compete with Jesus.

CONCLUSION

God's promises are God's answer to the war. Jesus is the demonstration of God's faithfulness. He lived every day knowing that the God of all creation was going to faithfully care for Him and provide for Him. God's faithfulness knew no bounds for Jesus: there was no situation, not even death, in which God would not be faithful. None. His Father would not fail Him.

The sufficiency of Jesus in the Eph 1 Diagram

That same degree of faithfulness is available for anyone who chooses to follow Jesus. God has made His promises available by grace. Man cannot earn, and desperately needs, the grace of

God. It is only by grace alone through Jesus alone that man can be lifted out of the valley of works and taken to the peak of God's presence. Everything begins to change as we learn to live and breathe in relationship with the Father, Son, and Holy Spirit.

In the next chapter we're going to work through four primary promises that God has made to us.

RESCUED PART 1: CHAPTER WORK

Begin your time in prayer. Meditate on the glory of God's faithfulness to all creation and to you. Breathe deeply again as you see yourself in God's presence. Bless Him with great joy at His revelation of grace and faithfulness. See Jesus' life as the perfect demonstration of grace-living that frees you to live the same. Write anything you think and/or feel here.

1. What are the struggles you have with believing in your Father's faithfulness?

2. In what areas of your life has God shown Himself faithful?

3. What is the relationship between God's faithfulness and personal suffering? If God is faithful, why do people suffer?

4. Why do you think it is challenging for you to receive grace from the Lord?

5. How does grace challenge your belief in your own ability to succeed in life?

6. What effects do you experience as you rest on Grace Mountain?

7. What are the specific mountains you climb or have climbed in your valley of works? What resulted? How does God's presence and promises surpass your valley life?

8. Read Philippians 3:2–11. What are the names, titles, and accomplishments you've earned in this life that you're now considering "rubbish" in light of Jesus?

Continue to work through the Eph 1. Now you can see the grace and faithfulness of your Father and the sufficiency of Jesus.

7: RESCUED PART 2

Ihope that you're continuing to awaken to the richness of life that comes from believing in God's unrelenting faithfulness. There is nothing you will ever be confronted with that falls outside of God's faithfulness and His promises. From disease, loss, tragedy, suffering, poverty and oppression to success, demonic attack, natural disasters, war, and even the end of the world, God is faithful.

No one is more powerful, dependable, or worthy. While your belief in God's provisions may waver and will be challenged, He will never fail. This is what Jesus breathed. This is what He taught His disciples. And this is what we are taught as well.

God has given us many specific promises throughout Scripture. In *The Way of Rest*, we focus on four. As His people, our Father has promised us love, freedom, rest, and power. The Almighty Creator of the universe has declared that if anyone will believe in Jesus, He will love them, set them free, give them rest, and empower them for life.

Guaranteed. No hesitation. No worry. No what-ifs.

Many times in following Jesus it can be difficult to know what God is doing and what His will is for our lives. However, because of His word, we have assurance that no matter what else is going on, He loves us, frees us, gives us rest, and empowers us. These are rich, fantastic promises that God continually fulfills in His people.

LOVE

Love is the greatest promise of God. It is the promise from which all other promises come.

Love is the motive of God:

- "For God so loved the world" (John 3:16).
- "But God demonstrates His love toward us in this" (Romans 5:8).

Whatever your conception is of God, it must begin with love. He is so filled with it that John wrote, "God is love" (1 John 4:10).

Do you remember when you first encountered the presence of God? What was it like for you? Many people remember a feeling of deep love they had never known before. They had experienced appetizers of love from others, but nothing with the purity, intensity, magnitude, completeness, and perfection as the love of God. The great news is that His promise of love was not just for your beginning but also for your whole journey. He gives you that taste of His love at first to encode love in the DNA of your relationship with Him.

You have and experience many riches from God's love. In the chapter on Trinitarian balance, we looked at the work of the Father, Son, and Holy Spirit in adopting you. Now we look at the reality that *you* are adopted. Paul writes in Galatians 4:5–6, "*We* might receive the adoption as sons. Because you are sons, God has sent for the Spirit of His Son into *our* hearts, crying, 'Abba! Father!'" (emphasis added). John 1:12 says, "But as many as received Him (Jesus), to them He gave the right to become children of God, even to those who believe in His name." Jesus teaches His disciples in Matthew 6:9 to begin their prayers, "Our Father who is in heaven." Because of His love, God the Father is not just God the Father—He is *your* Father.

Because He is now *your* Father, you are *His* child. You have a new identity. Whatever you were called before has died. You are now a child of God. This is who God says you are. Before you were a slave, an enemy, a sinner, a failure, and selfish and guilty and a whole host of other names. But now because of the promises of God, in Christ you are:

- A child of God (John 1:12)

- A royal priest (1 Peter 2:9)

- A new creation (2 Corinthians 5:17)

- A temple of the Holy Spirit (1 Corinthians 6:19–20)

- Blessed (Ephesians 1:3)

- Chosen (Matthew 22:14)

This is the glory of the love of God. Lifted out of the ashes of war, bruised, broken, and empty, you are filled with Divine Love, blessed with a new identity.

This new identity is not given because you performed for it. You were not good enough. As we read in Chapter 6, your new identity comes from God's promise to love you by grace. You are accepted by grace. You do not have to clean up or be right. God loves you where you are in the beginning, and He loves you where you are throughout your journey.

THE WAY OF REST:

One God

Two Kingdoms

Three Enemies

Four Promises:
Love, Freedom, Rest, and Power

Five Disciplines

In some ways the Internet has made relationships possible that were formerly impossible, or at least very difficult to maintain. Through programs like Skype, people can connect with, and many times see, family and friends they could only write to before. Because of His love promise in Jesus, man has the ability to connect with God in a way that wasn't possible before.

Your identity as a child is not some distant proclamation of a far-removed father. Your Father adopted you by sending His Spirit to live *in* you. As Jesus walked in the fullness of the Holy Spirit, so too does the one who follows Him. "But if the Spirit of Him who raised Jesus from the dead dwells in you, He who raised Christ Jesus from the dead will also give life to your mortal bodies through His Spirit who dwells in you" (Romans 8:11). The Galatians 4:1–7 adoption passage says, "God has sent forth the Spirit of His Son into our hearts." Because of God's love, you have intimacy with Him so that no matter how dark the night feels, how lonely the road may seem, or how deep the despair appears, you are *never* alone. That is a promise of your Father He will never fail to fulfill!

Because He loves by grace, you never have to fear being good enough. You never have to wonder if He is going to leave you. You never have to worry about being rejected. His promise of love gives you the security that life in the Valley of Works could never provide. It is an ongoing, lifelong promise that God will continually fulfill.

One additional benefit of God's love is the family He provides. When you're adopted, not only do you become sons and daughters, but you also get brothers and sisters.

Jesus said, 'Truly I say to you, there is no one who has left house of brothers or sisters or mother or father or children or farms, for My sake and for the gospel's sake, but that he will receive a hundred times as much now in the present age, houses and brothers and sisters and mothers and children and farms, along with persecutions; and in the age to come, eternal life (Mark 10:29–30).

For those who walk in Jesus' way, God has new families waiting who are full of His love. The great reality about these people is that they are all on the same journey you're on. They know. They understand. They get what life is like following the Lord in the reality of war. The fear of not belonging and people not caring leaves. Because the people of God are those who know what life is like in the war and were all formerly in their own sin, there's no fear of, "What are they going to think about me if they find out what I'm really like?" The people of God are all reformed and reforming sinners. Each has their own story of encountering God's transformational love. Grace abounds. When God's people gather together in the leading of the Holy Spirit, then the love of God is present and everyone experiences more fulfillment of God's promise to love.

Through adoption, identity, acceptance, security, intimacy, and family, God provides according to His promise of love. As His child, believe. Trust Him that He is good, loves you, and will lead you accordingly. Resting in His love puts you in a place to experience everything else He has for you.

If you then, being evil, know how to give good gifts to your children, how much more will your Father who is in heaven give what is good to those who ask Him! (Matthew 7:11).

FREEDOM

Freedom is love in action.[13] "In this is love, not that we loved God, but that He loved us and sent His Son to be the propitiation (the sacrifice which frees us) for our sins" (1 John 4:10). The glory of God can be seen in His efforts to set His people free! In light of the war and the deception of His enemies, God joyfully and powerfully overthrows His enemies in His people's lives. Our hope for life in the war explodes in light of God's presence to free His people.

Our Father has always worked to set His people free. Immediately after the fall of man in the Garden of Eden, when God cursed Satan, He said there would be a time when a future son would "bruise you (Satan) on the head." This bruising would be a deathblow to the reign and rule of Satan, eternally freeing those who walk with God. Later in the Old Testament, our Father raised up Moses to deliver Israel from their slavery to Egypt. "I have surely seen the affliction of My people who are in Egypt, and have given heed to their cry because of their taskmasters, for I am aware of their sufferings. So I have come to deliver them from the power of the Egyptians" (Exodus 3:7–8). In the book of Judges, our Father raised up Othniel, Ehud, Deborah, Gideon, and others to deliver Israel from their enemies and from their sin. Various words for "deliver," "save," and "rescue" are used 166 times in the Psalms.

> I love You, O Lord, my strength.
>
> The Lord is my rock and my fortress and my deliverer,
>
> My God, my rock, in who I take refuge;
>
> My shield and the horn of my salvation, my stronghold.
>
> I call upon the Lord, who is worthy to be praised,
>
> And I am saved from my enemies (Psalm 18:1–3).[14]

Prophets warn kings of coming bondage because of sin and then offer them deliverance through repentance. Freedom is a recurring promise throughout the Old Testament.

In the New Testament our Father sent Jesus, the prophesied son God spoke of when He cursed Satan, to be His ultimate deliverer. Jesus declares in Luke 4:16–18 that His mission is to set people free from bondage. Jesus spent His ministry forgiving sins, casting out demons, and training His disciples to identify and renounce the ways of the world. He freed those who would follow Him from the bondages of life. From the beginning of His preaching, Jesus proclaimed the availability of freedom. In Mark 1:15, Jesus declares in His first recorded sermon, "The time is fulfilled, and the kingdom of God is at hand; repent and believe in the Gospel." The Hebrew source of the Greek word, translated "gospel," was originally used to describe the news that messengers brought to the people whose army had won a war or battle. To have "gospel" is to declare that your side *has won*. From the beginning, Jesus has been declaring that the Kingdom of God has won!

The book of Revelation teaches us that Jesus will complete His victory in the last days. In the perfect timing of our Father, Jesus will return and end the reign of sin, the world, and Satan for good.

HOW FREEDOM WORKS

Freedom is possible because Jesus operates with greater authority and power than whatever binds you. Bondage and freedom are all about authority and power. The lies we believe, the anxiety we have, the pressure we feel, the loneliness we endure, the lust we indulge, and the jealousy that consumes us work because sin, the world, and Satan have real power in life. Their power is not to be trifled with or minimized. It has devastating, eternal consequences. Jesus is able to set us free because He is more powerful than they are. You can imagine three bullies ganging up on a person. A fourth person shows up and takes out the bullies, setting the person free!

We see in the Eph 1 diagram that Jesus has been raised *far* above all rule and principality. Where He sits is ridiculously higher than the height of the demonic, the world, and sin. Furthermore, the Eph 1 teaches us that *you are* raised and seated with Christ far above all rule, principality, the world, and sin. Freedom in Christ works when the surpassing power of Jesus, through the Holy Spirit, is unleashed on the far weaker powers of sin, the world, and Satan.

Freedom happens in two stages. In the first stage, freedom happens when you come to faith in Jesus. When you give your life to Jesus, the control of sin and Satan is broken in you. Paul says in Colossians 1:13–14, "For He rescued us from the domain of darkness, and transferred us to the kingdom of His beloved Son, in whom we have redemption, the forgiveness of sins." At salvation you have been delivered out of darkness and into light. You have been broken out of the eternal prison and adopted into the family of God! The sin you've been carrying has been forgiven—taken off your back—and has been replaced with the love, righteousness, and life of the Father, Son, and Holy Spirit. Many new believers will say, "I feel like the weight of the world has been taken off of me!" Freedom has come. New life has happened. Where there was thick, black, darkness there is now Light and Life.

The second stage of freedom happens as you continue to walk through life. Paul warns of the enslaving potential of new attacks in Galatians 5:1. "It was for freedom that Christ set us free; therefore keep standing firm and do not be subject again to a yoke of slavery." While you have been freed, the war still rages. Sin, the world, and Satan are still active forces in the world to steal everything God is doing. In 1 Peter 5:8, Peter warns those already following Jesus, "Be of sober spirit, be on the alert. Your adversary, the devil, prowls around like a roaring lion, seeking someone to devour." Freedom continues as you actively stand against the attacks of sin, the world, and Satan in the power of the Holy Spirit.

Through the transforming work of the Holy Spirit and your advancement in the Scripture, you will become increasingly sensitive to future temptations and attacks. In the beginning the war will be exhausting, "Am I really getting attacked this much?" You may feel like it is too much. You may want to quit. You will certainly want it to all go away. Take comfort from the reality that all of us who walk in the war feel this way! Realize that many of these thoughts are tactics of the enemy. This is the war! Trust the Lord. Let Him train you to walk in your authority.

Soon you will find that what once blindsided you and took you down for days or weeks you will now be able to overcome as the attack is happening. In the middle of a day, a person may be confronted with thoughts of despair as they consider their future. Instead of letting these thoughts develop, they immediately recognize the "fake duck," turns into it, and rebukes it with the greater power of Jesus. What before would have penetrated a life and done all sorts of damage simply falls to the ground defeated. Winning these types of battles throughout the day will be common for the one walking in the Way of Rest.

Because the battles happen throughout the day, Paul trains his disciples in 2 Corinthians 10:5 to take "every thought captive to the obedience of Christ." Peter trains his disciples to "prepare your minds for action, keep sober in spirit, fix your hope completely on the grace to be brought to you at the revelation of Jesus Christ" (1 Peter 1:13). Both men knew that sin, the world, and Satan target our minds and emotions, seeking to bind us. Even though we are seated with Christ and walking in His Spirit, we must engage in the war as He did. We cannot be passive and be free.

In addition to the daily attacks that threaten our freedom, we may also need to deal with unresolved issues from the past. The majority of freedom work we do involves resolving old wounds. One man experienced great disappointment from his perception that God was not faithful in a desperate time. Consequently, he said that if God was not going to come through for him, then he would serve Satan. He told Satan he would give his to life to him. Some years later he gave his life to Jesus. However, he never surrendered his satanic confession to the Lord. Consequently, he was tormented. Once he was willing to surrender what he had done and repent of it, the surpassing greatness of the power of Jesus easily broke the stranglehold this incident held.

One woman was sexually active in her late teens and early twenties. She came to faith at twenty-five and married at twenty-eight. She experienced intimacy issues in marriage as sex made her feel shameful and dirty. Even though she had given her life to Christ and was faithful in the Scriptures and church, she did not have freedom in this area of her life. She had never intentionally dealt with what she had done. Once she was willing to confess her sins of sexuality, their power was broken and she was freed.

The Apostle James writes in James 4:7, "Submit therefore to God. Resist the devil and he will flee from you." We can continually suffer because of unresolved issues when we do not submit them to the Lord. Issues in our lives not submitted to the Lord are like lit runways guiding the demonic into our lives. However, when we submit those areas to the Lord, not only will we have the authority and power of Jesus to repel the demonic, but we will also have the power to rebuke the enticements of our own sin.

In our discipleship we have found the most common areas of bondage to be sex, money, anger, unforgiveness, the occult, believing false teachings, and fear. Regardless of whether a person has given their life to Jesus, when past issues are unresolved they can still be binding. In the Eph 1 diagram, when a person comes to faith in Christ, a big, full "X" is placed over their former life, indicating the need to completely die and resolve all past issues. Jesus came to set us free from everything in our past so that we can live a new life.

Freedom is a promise of God. It is the heart of God. What father wants to see his sons or daughters languish in prison? "It is for freedom that Christ has set you free!" (Galatians 5:1). He sent Jesus to destroy the works of the evil one, overcome the world, and put sin under His feet so that we would not sit in the sin of negativity or pride. Jesus came so that we could sit atop Grace Mountain in the love of the Father, Son, and Holy Spirit and walk in the strength and power that is ours. When we surrender every area of our lives, we then experience the power of Christ blasting the power of darkness.

Jesus wins! We win!

REST

How many people do you know who live at rest? On Jesus' boat in Mark 4 it was one out of thirteen. Those statistics may be true today! Rest is a gift from God. It is the immediate effect of being set free. Rest, walking in the eternal peace of the Almighty God, is not only a promise of God, but it's also a distinguishing mark of a follower of Jesus. As Jesus lived at rest in the midst of war, so too will those who follow Him.

In Deuteronomy 28, Moses warns Israel of the consequences they will suffer if they do not trust the Lord. God is going to bring them into a land of great blessing, the Promised Land. However, if Israel proves unfaithful, God will remove them. In verses 64–66, Moses says,

> Moreover, the Lord will scatter you among all peoples, from one end of the earth to the other end of the earth; and there you shall serve other gods, wood and stone, which you or your fathers have not known. Among those nations you shall find no rest, and there will be no resting place for the sole of your foot; but there the Lord will give you *a trembling heart, failing eyes, and despair of soul. So your life shall hang in doubt before you; and you will be in dread night and day, and shall have no assurance of your life* (emphasis added).

Notice that the consequences the people suffer have a spiritual cause and come from not trusting God. People complaining of these things today would be medicated and enter into some kind of talk therapy when what they need is the love and faithfulness of God!

In contrast, look at the connection between freedom and rest in Judges 3:9–11:

> When the sons of Israel cried to the Lord, the Lord raised up a deliverer for the sons of Israel to deliver them, Othniel the son of Kenaz, Caleb's younger brother. The Spirit of the Lord came upon him, and he judged Israel. When he went out to war, the Lord gave Cushan-rishathaim king of Mesopotamia into his hand, so that he prevailed over Cushan-rishathaim. Then the land had rest forty years. And Othniel the son of Kenaz died.

Rest is a promise of God for those who follow Him. It is the internal result of freedom and victory. You do not rest because you have not allowed Jesus to overpower your enemies. When freedom happens, rest comes.

God made creation to exist at rest. *Stress was not a part of God's intent.* Once Adam and Eve fell, the world was no longer at rest. Instability became the norm. As a result, man has been on a quest for rest ever since. Not long after the time of Adam and Eve, a man named Lamech suffered under the constant toil of work. No matter how much he worked, he never found rest in his soul. He and his wife gave birth to a son. They named him Noah. Genesis 5:29 says, "Now he (Lamech) called his name Noah, saying, 'This one will give us rest from our work and from the toil of our hands arising from the ground which The Lord has cursed.'" The name "Noah" literally means rest. While many argue that life has never been as chaotic as it is today, Noah's name is evidence of the degree of unrest that has been in the world for thousands of years.

Noah became a precursor of the rest that Jesus would later show his disciples. In addition to Noah, God freed Israel from Egypt so that He could bring them to a resting place.

> You shall not do at all what we are doing here today, every man doing whatever is right in his own eyes; *for you have not as yet come to the resting place and the inheritance which the Lord your God is giving you.* When you cross the Jordan and live in the land which the Lord your God is giving you to inherit, and He gives you rest from all your enemies around you so that you live in security, then it shall come about that the place in which the Lord your God will choose for His name to dwell, there you shall bring all that I command you: your burnt offerings and your sacrifices, your tithes and the contribution of your hand, and all your choice votive offerings which you will vow to the Lord (Deuteronomy 12:8–11, emphasis added).

God has always been working to fulfill His promise of rest for those who will follow Him. In the life, ministry, and resurrection of Jesus, our Father took a great step in fulfilling His promise. As we saw in Chapter 1, the rest Jesus came to give was displayed in Mark 4:35–41. A life-threatening storm thrashed the boat that Jesus and the disciples were on in the Sea of Galilee. While the disciples feared for their lives, Jesus slept. He was at rest in the middle of their distress.

Jesus is the embodiment of grace, love, and freedom. He is the embodiment of rest. He is the master of rest. This is why Jesus is able to promise in Matthew 11:28–30,

> Come to Me, all who are weary and heavy-laden, and I will give you rest. Take My yoke upon you and learn from Me, for I am gentle and humble in heart, and you will find rest for your souls. For My yoke is easy and My burden is light.

The rest man has earnestly sought since the fall of man was and is now being offered through Jesus. What man could never achieve through any of his own efforts, whether individual or collective, has been made available by the grace of God through the sufficient work of Jesus. As you believe in everything God has revealed in the Eph 1 diagram and practice the disciplines Jesus walked in, you will continually experience divine rest. In the pattern of Israel, God pursues you because He loves you. As God delivered Israel from the bondage of Egypt, He delivers you from the bondages of sin, the world, and Satan. Freed from captivity, you will experience His rest that comes from walking in His faithfulness. At rest, you are filled with His promised power, equipped to continue to walk in victory and train others to do the same.

POWER

Because of the promises of God, you can walk in the power of Jesus Christ. Consider that reality for a moment. The same power that worked in Jesus' life is available for you. No one has to live in fear. No one has to stay a victim. There is no self-pity and no power that can keep you down. God has promised His power to His people. This is fantastic news to those who know the brutality of the war and who want to be used by the King to do His work.

Throughout the Old Testament the power of God is poured on and through the people of God. God parted the Red Sea through Moses. Because of Joshua's faithfulness the walls of

Jericho fell. God used Gideon's army of three hundred to defeat a much larger force so that everyone would know God won the war. God gave power to David as he slew Goliath and gave power to Elijah against the Baal prophets on Mount Carmel. Isaiah, Jeremiah, Ezekiel, Hosea, Zachariah, and the prophets all spoke in the power of God. The Old Testament shows a very powerful God actively involved in His people, working His power in them and through them. Jesus, of course, is the embodiment of God's power. We have already seen how Jesus' power is Holy-Spirit, Kingdom power. He came filled with the Spirit to re-establish the Kingdom of God, gaining victory over sin, the world, and Satan. In that, He had the power to stay pure, develop godly character, be faithful to His Father's will, share the Gospel, heal the sick, cast out demons, and command nature. Jesus had a degree of power no one had ever seen before.

After Jesus, the power of God continued in His people. On the day of Pentecost, the Holy Spirit was poured out on the disciples according to God's promise.[15] Filled with the Holy Spirit, the disciples were changed from fear-filled and uncertain people to bold witnesses for the Lord. The preached, healed, cast out demons, endured persecution, traveled to foreign lands, were martyred, loved each other, worshipped, served, lived holy, and followed the will of God. Because of God's power in their lives, many others came to faith in Christ and God was glorified.

This same power of God is available to you today. Jesus taught His disciples in John 14:12, "Truly, truly, I say to you, he who believes in Me, the works that I do, he will do also; and greater works than these he will do; because I go to the Father." Jesus saw a future when all of His disciples, including you, would be empowered to do greater works than He had done. You no longer have to live in your own strength. You no longer have to strain against the war of the day. You no longer have to be a victim or drown in self-pity. The power of God is available to you today. To walk in the Way of Rest is to walk in the power of Jesus.

In fact, rest happens in part because we know the power that we have, and we know how to use it. You've seen action movies or have read stories where the hero calmly walks into a room full of bad guys. The hero has no anxiety. His rest does not come from the absence of attack. He's about to fight. Rather, his rest comes because he knows *how* to fight. He knows he has greater ability than those around him.

The key to the power of God is intimacy with God. We never seek power; we seek intimacy and power is there. Scripture teaches us that the power of God is in the person of the Holy Spirit. Look at the direct connection between the Holy Spirit and power in Jesus' words in Acts 1:8: "But you will receive power when the Holy Spirit comes upon you; and you shall be my witnesses both in Jerusalem, and in all Judea and Samaria, and even to the remotest part of the earth." Again, Jesus says in John 14:16,

> I will ask the Father, and He will give you another Helper, that He may be with you forever; that is the Spirit of truth, whom the world cannot receive, because it does not see Him or know Him, but you know Him because He abides with you and will be in you.

Do you see that the power of God comes through intimacy with the Spirit of God? The Holy Spirit will be in the disciples of Jesus. What is He coming into the disciples to do? The same things, and greater things, than He did in Jesus. Whereas in the Old Testament the Holy Spirit came *on* God's people to do God's work, in the New Testament and in your life the Holy Spirit comes *in* God's people. Now that Jesus has taken sin away, the Holy Spirit can come into your life. As you develop intimacy with Him you will experience His power, God's power.

There are *many* empowering works of the Holy Spirit in you. Timothy hit a low point in his ministry. He was worn out and considering quitting. The Apostle Paul wrote 2 Timothy to encourage him in the Lord to stay in the fight. He wrote in 2 Timothy 1:7, "For God has not

127

given us a spirit of timidity, but of power and love and discipline." The Holy Spirit works in the spirits of people to make the timid bold. He changes dispositions. He also works in people's lives to produce godly character in them. Galatians 5:22–23 says, "But the fruit of the Spirit is love, joy, peace, patience, kindness, goodness, faithfulness, gentleness, self-control." Godly character is not attained by striving to be a good person. Godly character is a work of the Holy Spirit in a person surrendered to His power.

Furthermore, the Holy Spirit empowers God's people to succeed in the roles God has for them. Ephesians 5:22–6:4 gives God's word to husbands, wives, and parents. The direction is beautiful! However, Ephesians 5:22–6:4 is predicated on Ephesians 1:1–2:10, which says that followers of Jesus are blessed with every "spiritual blessing" in the heavenly places, are powered by the Holy Spirit, and are saved by grace. God does not expect His people to have great marriages and families on their own. He expects them to surrender to the Holy Spirit and, by grace, be Spirit-blessed and empowered to succeed in every role in life. Life in the promises has no pressure to perform.

In the same way, evangelism is also a work of the Holy Spirit. Certainly, according to Acts 1:8, the Holy Spirit works to empower people to share the Gospel with others. Paul shares his secret to effective evangelism in 2 Corinthians 2:4. "My message and my preaching were not in persuasive words of wisdom, but in demonstration of the Spirit and power, so that your faith would not rest on the wisdom of men, but on the power of God." Paul trained followers of Jesus to rest their faith on the power of God! The effectiveness of Paul's ministry was not based on his knowledge or his personality but on the Holy Spirit and His power! So there is no pressure on you to win the world or your neighbor. Be faithful to the leading of the Spirit and let Him loose.

We also see in Acts 1:8 that the Holy Spirit empowers people to be faithful to go where God leads them. Jesus says that the disciples will bear witness to Him in "Jerusalem, all Judea,

Samaria, and even to the remotest part of the earth." God had a plan for sending His people with His Gospel powered by the Holy Spirit all over the world. The Holy Spirit enables you to faithfully follow God's Kingdom plan for your life.

Notice how in 2 Thessalonians 1:11–12 Paul's belief in the empowering work of the Holy Spirit shapes the way he prays:

> To this end also we pray for you always, that our God will count you worthy of you calling, and fulfill every desire for goodness and the work of faith with power (from the Holy Spirit), so that the name of our Lord Jesus will be glorified in you, and you in Him, according to the grace of our God and the Lord Jesus Christ.

You are not called to walk out God's will for your life in your power. You don't have the ability to do it. You're called to walk out God's will for your life in the power of the Holy Spirit. The Holy Spirit also enables you to live holy and to overcome sin and the world. Paul trains his disciples in Romans 8:13, "For if you are living according to the flesh, you must die; but if by the Spirit you are putting to death the deeds of the body, you will live." 1 John 5:4 says, "For whatever is born of God overcomes the world; and this is the victory that has overcome the world—our faith."[16]

Furthermore, the power of the Holy Spirit enables God's people to heal the sick and cast out demons (Luke 9:1–2), build up the body by using specific gifts the Spirit gives (1 Corinthians 12–14), and endure persecution (1 Peter 4:14).

Finally, the Holy Spirit works to create communities of God's people. Acts 2:41 says that on the day of Pentecost, after Peter had preached in the power of the Spirit, about three thousand people were added to the Kingdom. Acts 2:42 records what their new community looked like: "They were continually devoting themselves to the apostles' teaching and to fellowship, to the breaking of bread and to prayer." These were not programs of the church; these were demonstrations of the power of the Holy Spirit. I am continually perplexed by churches seeking to program these things when the Scripture says they are organic works of the Holy Spirit. As followers of Jesus we do not have to try and do these things. We have to surrender to the Spirit and let His power do what He wants.

All of this should be fantastic news to you. The promise of the power of the Holy Spirit means you do not have to do and cannot do even if you wanted to. Faithfulness to God, intimacy with God, feeling great about yourself, and victory in the war are not reserved for those with great personalities, deep reservoirs of knowledge, pastors, or the wealthy. All of these blessings of God are yours because of Jesus' work on the cross and the outpouring of the Holy Spirit. God says through grace, "You can't, I CAN!" I join my prayers to those of Paul for all of us from Ephesians 1:18–19, "I pray that the eyes of your heart may be enlightened so that you will know . . . what is the surpassing greatness of His power toward us who believe."

CONCLUSION

More than just the promise of power, all the promises of God—love, freedom, rest and more— are yours by *grace*. And it is the will of the Almighty Father of all creation that you have them. He has been orchestrating His cosmological plan to reconcile you to Him so that you can have intimacy with Him and enjoy His promises in this life and the next. It is the will of God that you have these and it is a work of the Holy Spirit that you experience them!

All of the promises of God are manifestations of intimacy with God. Never put the promises before His presence. Never make your intimacy conditional on the promises. You spend time with the Father, Son, and Holy Spirit because of who they are. All of the promises and blessings will flow organically and abundantly as you love the Lord your God with your all your mind, body, soul, and strength.

Jesus' Kingdom way, the Way of Rest, is life lived in intimacy with God, trusting Him to be faithful to His gracious promises. It is a life freed of self, believing that your Father has your life and everything in your life taken care of. These are His "precious and magnificent promises" through which we "become partakers of the divine nature, having escaped the corruption that is in the world by lust" (2 Peter 1:4).

RESCUED PART 2: CHAPTER WORK

Start your time in prayer thanking your Father for the content of His promises. Thank Him for His love, freedom, rest, and power. Thank Jesus for making them all possible by grace. Thank the Holy Spirit for His faithfulness to apply these in you. What a blessing! As you see yourself on Grace Mountain in the presence of the Father, Son, and Holy Spirit, see them with their promises. Write anything you think and/or feel here.

In this chapter work you are going to spend time reflecting on each of the four promises and the implications of each in your life. Take your time. Do not rush. Allow the Holy Spirit to show you new truths about each.

1. Love: Spend time reflecting on your adoption. God is your Father. You are His child. You have a new identity. Your old names are dead. You are secure. You no longer have to perform to be accepted. As the Spirit moves this around in you, write what you are thinking and/or feeling.

2. Freedom: Are there any areas of bondage, or any places where the enemies of God have done damage, where Jesus wants to heal you? What kind of images do you receive when you consider the reality that you're free? Are there hidden places you do not like to go where the Lord is asking you to trust Him to walk with you into them?

3. Rest: What images does the Spirit give you regarding God's promise of rest? How much does Jesus' rest promise in Matthew 11:28–30 affect you? How does it help you that He says He is "gentle and humble in heart" in that invitation?

4. Power: How does your power in Jesus change your perspective of yourself? Not only are you a child of God, but you are a Spirit-empowered child of God. What are the roles in your life where you need to actively depend on God's power? No matter how much power you're operating in, Paul still prays that you will know more the power of God. Ask the Lord to show you more of His power toward you. Are there other areas of your life where you need His power?

Keep working the Eph 1. Now you're seeing the specifics of Jesus' work in your life. The Eph 1 is becoming an increasingly powerful tool of clarity for you.

BE

THE WAY OF REST

8: TRAINING

In previous chapters we've looked at the foundations of what Jesus believed. He believed in an involved Trinitarian God, a war between two kingdoms, three aggressive enemies, and promises from God for life. Now we'll look at how those beliefs shaped His practices. As discussed in the chapter on organics, a direct connection exists between what Jesus believed and what He practiced. What did Jesus do in light of what He believed? What were His responsibilities in His relationship with God? Did He do things in certain ways that we need to learn?

It's helpful to see that Jesus *trains* His disciples to walk with Him. Many of us are *taught* things we never use. How often in school did you think, "I'm never going to use this in my life"? Jesus never taught His disciples anything He did not intend for them to use. In His day, to teach was to train. Jesus trained His disciples. He equipped them with specific beliefs and practices for them to effectively use.

So what were His practices?

In the Way of Rest, we focus on five categories of disciplines. Throughout His life, Jesus practiced reflection, releasing, receiving, resisting, and responding. In these practices Jesus experienced deep intimacy with His Father and the Holy Spirit, learned God's word for His life, stood against any temptation to disobedience, and faithfully followed God's will. Then He trained His disciples to do the same. His disciples' writings to the next generation of followers contain very specific techniques in each of these categories. The next generation began to learn them and was charged with training a new generation. Disciples were making disciples.

Let's work through each discipline, explaining each and giving specific techniques.

REFLECTION

Reflection is the foundation of all Jesus' disciplines. Reflection is being continuously, consciously engaged in a relationship with the Father, Son, and Holy Spirit. Marriage provides a great analogy for reflection. A spouse lives throughout the day easily aware that he or she is married. Fluidly, without having to manufacture anything, a husband or wife thinks about their spouse during the day. Their relationship is always present. Furthermore, their marriage shapes every decision they make: financial, career, time, family, vacation, or other. This is reflective living.

Jesus' relationship with God was always present. Jesus *never* forgot that He was the Son of God. Jesus *never* lost sight of His Father's faithfulness. He always lived in the power of the Holy Spirit. And every decision He made in His life was determined by His relationship with God. Can you see the power of reflective living? Can you imagine how your life would change if you lived every moment aware that you're a child of God who is eternally faithful to you in all things? That's intense!

The goal of reflection is intimacy. The various techniques of reflection all serve to cultivate intimacy with God. Reflection is never about the technique; it's always about love and connection with the Lord. Being is more important than doing. We reflect on who He is and who we are. In reflection, we are not concerned about what He has for us.

A little boy wakes up in the morning, runs to his dad, and jumps in his lap. The boy asks, "Daddy, what do you want me to do today? What do you have?" The dad looks at his son with the warmest eyes and replies, "Son, all I want you to do right now is sit in my lap and let me love you. Be my son. There will be things to do but, for now, sit with me." This is reflection—just being in the presence of God.

THE WAY OF REST:

One God

Two Kingdoms

Three Enemies

Four Promises

Five Disciplines: Reflection, Releasing, Receiving Resisting, and Responding

Jesus trains His disciples to abide, His language for reflecting. "I am the Vine, you are the branches; he who abides in Me and I in him, bears much fruit, for apart from Me you can do nothing" (John 15:5). We looked at this in organics: abiding is a natural practice for one who identifies themselves as a branch to Jesus' vine. The branch rests in its connection to the vine. Abiding (reflecting) is the default position of the branch. Abiding is the posture the branch was created to live in!

Look at the specificity of training in reflection Paul gives the disciples at Philippi: "Finally, brethren, whatever is true, whatever is honorable, whatever is right, whatever is pure, whatever is lovely, whatever is of good repute, if there is any excellence and if anything worthy of praise, *dwell* on these things" (Philippians 4:8, emphasis added). Peter trains us in 1 Peter 1:13, "Therefore, prepare your minds for action, keep sober in spirit, *fix your hope* completely on the grace to be brought to you at the revelation of Jesus Christ" (emphasis added). These men trained disciples to reflect deeply on all things in their relationships with God.

You may also think of reflecting as soaking. Early in my marriage my wife showed me the power of soaking dishes. I would scrub a plate hard to remove every food stain. She showed me that if I will simply let the dish soak in water, all the food stains will just fall off. Soaking is the power of reflecting! You soak in the love, faithfulness, grace, and mercy of God. Just be in Him.

Abiding, dwelling, fixing, and soaking are all different ways of describing the discipline of reflection. Let's work through some specific techniques.

REFLECTING TECHNIQUES

PRAYER

Jesus used prayer as a means of reflecting on His Father. In the opening of the Lord's Prayer, Jesus trains His disciples to pray, "Our Father, who is in Heaven." He wants His disciples to reflect on the nature of who God is and who they are. He is their Father who lovingly adopted them. They are His children. He sent His Spirit into their hearts crying, "Abba, Father!" He is responsible for providing and leading them. He is their Father who is in Heaven. He reigns over all creation. Reflect on the magnitude of who your Father is. In the beginning, your Father created the heavens and the earth.

In reflective prayer we take very specific attributes of God and soak in them. You may reflect on His love or His mercy, His faithfulness or His judgment. In reflective prayer you are not rushed for time or hurrying to get to another part of your prayer. You sit in His presence. You can also soak in what He says about you. Fix your mind on the reality that you are a child of God. You are no longer whoever you used to be. Again, the goal in reflective prayer is intimacy.

Reflective prayer is something you do every day. Pray in the morning, spending time with God by yourself. As part of your prayer, reflect. Soak in different aspects of God's love and faithfulness. Then, use reflective prayer throughout the day. As you look at the list of things you have to accomplish, reflect on God's wisdom and power. If you have children, reflect on God's favor in blessing you with them. As you review your finances, reflect on the longtime faithfulness of God. Your prayer does not have to be long. You will be blessed by how small reflections during the day serve to keep you walking in the way of Jesus.

BIBLE-READING

Spending time in God's word for the purposes of reflecting is powerful. As you read the Scriptures, a verse, story, image or feeling may move you. Stop what you're doing and soak in it. Reflect and allow the Holy Spirit to take what He is giving you deeper and deeper in you. Do not be in a hurry to move on.

Bible-reading is something you do daily. As your new relationship with God shapes your days, you change how you spend your time and create space in the morning to pray and read the Word. While there are different ways to read the Bible, I always train people to start at the beginning of a book and read it through to the end. Let that be your main technique of Bible-reading. Devotionals and Bible studies are great, but there's no substitute for starting at the beginning of a book and reading. Move from one genre to another, from the poetry of Psalms to the letters of Paul. Move from the Old Testament to the New Testament. If what you're reading is getting "dry," don't quit reading, just move on to a different book.

Be careful with Bible-reading plans that you do not move away from what God is doing in you just to stay up with your reading plan. As you grow in your faith, develop more sophisticated reading techniques. Move from reading to using book outlines, historical studies, and word studies that will continue to deepen your relationship with the Lord. Always be aware of the danger of knowledge!

JOURNALING

Writing down what you're experiencing is a very helpful way to reflect. If you think about the wonders of God as a series of beautiful locations on a map, journaling will help you see how one location leads to another. For example, if you're reflecting on the faithfulness of God in Joseph's life, you'll take in everything that location has to offer. In a corner of that location, you'll notice a path you hadn't seen before. As you walk down that path, you'll discover the strength Joseph had because of God's faithfulness in his life. You'll see how active Joseph's faith was even while unjustly imprisoned. Journaling will allow you to see what one "location" has and how it connects to another.

BREATHING

This one may sound odd, but it's a powerful technique for every category in the Way of Rest. The actual word for the Holy Spirit in the Old Testament is the Hebrew word, "Breath." The Holy Spirit is likened to the breath of God. Job 33:4 says, "The Spirit of God has made me, and the breath of the Almighty gives me life."

In reflection you learn to breathe deeply. You want your breath to be in rhythm with God's breath, the Holy Spirit. As you take in deep breaths and release them, you will feel yourself relax. Your mind will slow down. You'll be able to focus on specific things. Breathing is a great technique you can use throughout the day. Before you pick up the kids, have a difficult conversation with a spouse, walk into a meeting, or follow the Lord and forgive someone, take a few deep breaths while reflecting on the love of your Father and watch what happens! Breathing is also effective as you draw away to be alone with the Lord. Take as many deep breaths as you'd like. Each time you may feel like you've reached the point the Lord has for you. Then you breathe again and discover there is more!

MUSIC

Songs are recorded from Genesis to Revelation (See Exodus 15:1–18 and Revelation 4:5–11). Music was a powerful tool for people to remember who God is and what He has done. Listening to songs that describe various attributes of God can be an intense way of reflecting on the Lord. And this can be done all through the day. Depending on your work, you can even do this while you're working. Be careful that people aren't around when you break out into song! These are some of the reflecting techniques Jesus and His disciples used. Notice that these are specific techniques that can be learned, mastered, and taught to others. I encourage you to practice and grow in all of them.

RELEASING

Releasing is the discipline of surrendering specific issues to the Lord. The key in releasing is to properly identify the issues within. Paul trains his disciples in Philippians 4:6–7 when he states, "Be anxious for nothing, but in everything by prayer and supplication with thanksgiving let your requests be made known to God. And the peace of God, which surpasses all comprehension, will guard your hearts and your minds in Christ Jesus."

Paul exhorts disciples to be anxious about nothing. Anxiety reveals a lack of trust in God's faithfulness. In releasing, you identify those sources of anxiety and surrender them to the Lord, believing He is faithful in them. (For that matter, you also release sources of fear, jealousy, greed, and other forms of darkness). If you release properly, you may come into prayer with anxiety, but you will leave with the peace of God.

Paul's practice is built on Jesus' training. In Matthew 6:25–34, Jesus teaches through a list of areas that can cause anxiety, like food, clothing, and drink. Throughout this passage, Jesus tells His followers not to worry about these things. He specifies areas that can cause negativity in a person's life. He frees people from anxiety by directing them to focus on the faithfulness of their Father to provide.

> "For the Gentiles eagerly seek all these things; for your Heavenly Father knows that you need all these things. But seek first His kingdom and His righteousness, and all these things will be added to you" (Matthew 6:32-33).

Releasing happens throughout the day, all day, every day. By releasing, you will learn to take responsibility for your thoughts and emotions and better understand how to control them. Specific issues you hold on to are identified so that you can turn them over to the Lord. Let's work through some releasing techniques.

RELEASING TECHNIQUES

LISTENING TO THE HOLY SPIRIT

All releasing is listening to the Holy Spirit. In the other releasing techniques we'll work through, the Holy Spirit speaks through different means. In this technique, the Holy Spirit speaks directly to you to make known issues you need to surrender.

As you pray, ask the Lord to show you issues you're holding on to. Allow the Spirit to show you what He wants to show you. Then, take what He shows you and surrender to the Lord. "Father, in the name of Jesus, I release my fear/anxiety/guilt about _____ to you. I declare that you are faithful in _____. Amen."

BIBLE STUDY

Through your study of the Word, the Holy Spirit will show you a root issue. When the issue is exposed, take authority over each issue and release it to the Lord in the prayer just given.

DISCIPLESHIP

The Holy Spirit will regularly use other people to speak into your life to help you identify areas in which you need to surrender. Surrounding yourself with trusted brothers and sisters in the Lord who are veterans in the Way is a wise move. God has made us to need each other. Receiving the benefit of others' insight is a valuable way of discovering issues within. When issues are exposed, take authority over each issue and release it according to the prayer above.

JOURNALING

Journaling is another powerful tool of clarity. Through journaling, what seems like a jumbled mess of thoughts or feelings will take form. The Holy Spirit always works to help you through your issues. When you start, your journaling may look like a train wreck. Let it be a mess. Get it all out. Then let the Spirit begin to bring the clarity you need. As He identifies root issues then surrender them to the Lord.

Notice again in Paul's training from Philippians 4:6–7 that you will come into prayer with anxiety yet leave with peace. You'll know that you have released the issues causing your instability when you have peace. Paul defines this peace as something you will not be able to explain—it surpasses all understanding. The peace will come from God and will guard your heart and your mind. Why does the peace of God need to guard anything, let alone your heart and mind? Because you live at war! And the enemies of your life actively attack your peace in the Lord. Two of their access points are your thoughts and emotions. In releasing, you actively clean out your heart and mind while God posts His peace at your gates. If you don't have peace, there's more to release!

RECEIVING

Jesus was not a manufacturer; He was a distributor. He did not give out of what He created. He gave out of what He received. Therefore, He had no pressure to create, to perform, or to produce. Jesus continuously gave out of what He received. "Truly, truly I say to you, the Son can do nothing of Himself, unless it is something He sees the Father doing; for whatever the Father does, these things the Son also does in like manner" (John 5:19). "I glorified You on the earth, having accomplished the work which You have given Me to do" (John 17:4). "The Spirit of the Lord is upon Me, because He anointed Me to preach the Gospel to the poor" (Luke 4:18). Jesus did not create or manufacture anything in His life. His Kingdom recipe, the Way of Rest, is a life of being and giving out of what is received.

Scripture uses three images that illustrate this receiving life. Disciples are called sheep and the Lord is the Shepherd (Psalm 23, John 10:1–18). Disciples are called branches and the Lord is the Vine (John 15:1–5). And disciples are called clay and the Lord is the Potter (Isaiah 29:16, Romans 9:19–26). All of these images illustrate the dependent nature of the relationship between God and man. Notice that God *wants* to be your supply! That is the position He loves to have (and is the only position He will have). Look at Paul's confidence in God's supply for you: "And my God will supply all your needs according to His riches in Christ Jesus" (Philippians 4:19). You need to stand on this and declare it!

Therefore, as followers of Jesus in the Way of Rest, you are not responsible for being great spouses, parents, friends, employees, employers, or children of God. You do not manufacture your efforts in any area of life. You are freed from performing. You become who God is leading you to be and do what God is leading you to do. You live receiving, not producing.

The glory of God is seen in that He supplies you with greater material than you could ever create. God will make you a greater spouse, parent, friend, employee, or employer than you could ever be on your own. By letting Him supply, you will experience the wonder of His presence, wisdom, transformation, love, power, and leading in every area of your life. Now you are a God-filled mom or dad, a God-filled spouse, and a God-filled friend. This is the glory of branch-living!

The key to receiving is living in a state of need. Unfortunately, being dependent is often equated with weakness. I have walked many people through John 15:5. They love the portion that says, "I am the Vine and you are the branches." That sounds good. But they bristle at the end of the verse: "Apart from Me you can do nothing." Here comes the pushback and the struggle. People are good with the positive aspect of being a branch: Jesus supplies. But they don't like the negative aspect of it: apart from the vine you can do nothing. Jesus does not hide from this requirement of receiving. To receive is to be dependent on someone else's supply. As you practice the discipline of reflection and meditate on God's love and faithfulness, your belief about dependence will change and you will learn the great joy of looking to the Lord in all things.

Understanding that an attitude of dependence is most important in receiving, let's work through some specific techniques.

RECEIVING TECHNIQUES

PRAYER

All receiving is a work of the Holy Spirit. Supplying you is His responsibility. In prayer, the Holy Spirit speaks directly to you and supplied whatever He wants you to have. As you pray, make sure you create space to listen. Do not let your prayer be filled with your talking. Learn to be silent. When you find your mind racing with other thoughts, practice releasing. Identify each thought swirling around and release them to the Lord. Now, be still. Ask the Lord to speak. It's helpful to ask as specifically as you can. Do not ask, "Lord, what do I need to do for you to bless me?" Ask,

"Father, I need to know how to talk to my spouse about this issue we're having. Will you give me direction?" Or, "Father, we need your wisdom in parenting our child through this issue. Give us direction in what we should do." Ask specifically. Be still. Let Him speak.

Acts 10:9–16 details a time when Peter was praying and the Holy Spirit gave him a dream, showing him God's will for a specific situation. In your prayers the Holy Spirit can use imagery, passages of Scripture, memories, and whatever else He wants in order to speak to you. Be open, ask, and listen.

BIBLE STUDY

The Bible is a powerful way to receive from the Lord. God has given His Word to you so that you can receive from Him. It's a long book—He's given plenty to receive through it! As you study, God will give you His direction. Paul writes in 2 Timothy 3:16–17, "All Scripture is inspired by God and profitable for teaching, for reproof, for correction, for training in righteousness, so that the man of God may be adequate, *equipped for every good work*" (emphasis added).

In addition to regular time in the Scripture, there are almost an unlimited amount of Bible studies available on every topic imaginable. Be careful in what studies you do as not all studies are good, and none are inspired in the way Scripture is. Use these studies to supplement your Scripture-reading, not to take its place.

DISCIPLESHIP

Allowing veterans in the Lord to speak into your life provides deep reservoirs of wisdom that will greatly benefit you. There is nothing you're enduring or need direction in that other brothers and sisters have not walked in and through. God is so beautifully faithful to bring others into our journeys. Seek them out. If you do not see any such veterans where you are, pray that God will bring them into your life. Seek their wisdom. Receive from the Holy Spirit through them.

While God has stopped writing Scripture, He continues to speak in many different ways to many different people. As followers of Jesus, we cultivate the ability to receive from the Lord when we learn to depend on Him, to listen to Him, and to walk in specifics.

Learning to hear and discern the voice of the Lord can be challenging. I remember learning the sound of my wife's voice before we were married. She had a roommate whose voice sounded just like hers! However, the longer we dated the easier it was to distinguish the two. As you spend time with God in His Word and in prayer, it will become easier to distinguish His voice. So far we have worked through the disciplines of reflection, releasing, and receiving. All three of these can be seen in Psalm 94:17–19:

If the Lord had not been my help, my soul would soon have dwelt in the abode of silence. If I should say, 'My foot has slipped,' Your loving-kindness, O Lord, will hold me up. When my anxious thoughts multiply within me, Your consolations delight my soul.

After receiving God's Word we must learn how to resist the forces of sin, the world, and Satan that actively war against our faithfulness.

RESISTING

You have to see this. In the Garden of Eden, Adam and Eve walked with God in the cool of the day. They saw God as no other has, except Jesus. God gave them His word for their lives. They had it all! Then the enemy came, the master deceiver, and led them away. They sinned. They did the one thing God told them not to do. They immediately experienced the consequences of their sin. Naked and ashamed, they hid from God.

ARGH! What happened? How did they fall so badly?

They were in relationship with God. They knew His word for their lives. So how did they fall so far so fast?

They didn't fight. They did not stand firm in their faith and resist the attacks of the enemy. There's no possible or negotiable way to live in the way of Jesus' rest unless you learn to resist sin, the world, and Satan. Jesus fought. His disciples fought. Their disciples fought. Everyone who perseveres in the Lord fights. Resisting is the discipline of fighting against your sin, the world, and Satan so that you can obey the words you have received.[17]

Genesis 4:1–8 tells the story of Cain and Abel. Both brothers brought an offering to God. He was pleased with Abel's but not with Cain's. Cain was furious. Maybe the enemy put images in his mind of Abel having "favorite" status. Maybe the enemy was not involved at all, and Cain seethed with jealousy all on his own. Nevertheless, God knew Cain's heart and warned him in verse 7, "If you do not do well (in handling your jealousy), sin is crouching at the door, and its desire is for you, *but you must master it*" (emphasis added). God was training Cain to fight. Cain failed. He gave in and murdered his brother. He didn't fight!

Satan came to tempt Jesus in Luke 4:1–13. He tempted Jesus with three different, very specific lies. Jesus resisted each one by declaring specific, appropriate truth. Luke 4:13 says, "When the devil had finished every temptation, he left Him until an opportune time." Paul trains disciples in Ephesians 6:10–11: "Finally, be strong in the Lord and in the strength of His might. Put on the full armor of God, so that you will be able to stand firm against the schemes of the devil."

He writes in Colossians 2:8, "See to it that no one takes you captive through philosophy and empty deception, according to the tradition of men, according to the elementary principles of the world, rather than according to Christ." James 4:7 states, "Submit therefore to God. Resist the devil and he will flee from you." Every New Testament letter has content on training disciples how to fight against sin, the world, and Satan. Many, many Christians suffer unnecessarily because they do not know how to fight.

Remember that God has promised you power. As you walk intimately with Him, you will know that you have been raised and seated with Christ far above all rule and principality. His authority is your authority. His power is your power. Resisting is all about exercising your Christ-given authority and power against the lies of sin, the world, and Satan.

In each of the disciplines we have stressed the importance of specifics. Resisting is no different. In the middle of your day the enemy may introduce an image of you with a body shape that's more "culturally attractive." Sin is at your door. You may feel depression try to access your heart. Instead of giving in to the temptation, you turn into it, just like Jesus turned into the storm on the boat in Mark 4:31–35. You turn into that lie. You do not receive it. You resist it in the name of Jesus, declaring, "I am a child of the Living God who loves me. I reject this lie in the name of Jesus." That lie falls to the ground and dies. Instead of giving in and suffering depression because you don't think you look like what's culturally accepted, you experience great joy in the love and approval of the God of All Creation.

Jesus trains His disciples in Matthew 5:21–47 on how to deal with the specific sins of anger, adultery, divorce, lying, revenge, and favoritism. These are specific areas in which we can be attacked.

This same scenario of attack-resist can happen many times throughout a day. The presence or absence of attacks is secondary. What's primary is intimacy with God. If the enemy cannot trip you on a specific attack, he will try to wear you down by getting you to focus on the fight. Remember, the goal of the enemy is to get your eyes off of the love and faithfulness of the Father, Son, and Holy Spirit. Resisting works when you stand against everything that pulls you away from intimacy with God.

RESISTANCE TECHNIQUES

BE PREPARED.

If you're not prepared to fight, you've already lost. If you believe that you're not under attack or that somehow you will be able to handle whatever may come up on your own, you're done. It's just a matter of time. At times, the New Testament authors scream, "BE READY!" Paul says in Ephesians 6:10–11, "Be strong in the Lord and in the strength of His might. Put on the full armor of God, so that you will be able to stand firm against the schemes of the devil." Peter trains in 1 Peter 1:13, "Prepare your minds for action." Jude says in Jude 1:3, "Contend earnestly for the faith." Walking in Jesus' Kingdom way is a call to arms! When Jesus trains His disciples to daily pray, "Your kingdom come," He's training them to be awake and prepared for the war.

While we're not called to be fixated on the war, we are called to be fixed on Jesus, and to be aware and ready to fight. Every day you get up, part of your time with the Lord should be spent preparing yourself for the reality of war. Therefore, when the attacks come you're not caught off guard, whining, or being a victim.

REJECT SPECIFICALLY.

This is the core of resistance. Reject specific lies with specific truth in the authority of Jesus. Now, resistance comes after reflection, releasing, and receiving, so it's predicated on walking in the Spirit. Paul trains in Galatians 5:16, "But I say, walk by the Spirit, and you will not carry out the misdeeds of the flesh." The reason you will not carry out the misdeeds of the flesh is because in the Spirit you are empowered to strike them down as you are tempted. As we have seen, James equips disciples in James 4:10, "Submit yourself to the Lord, resist the devil, and he will flee from you." Submission to the Lord is the discipline of releasing. In releasing you're continuously submitting very specific areas of your life to the Lord. Therefore, when the fiery dart comes, you're able to resist the devil and he must flee from you.

Your ability to successfully resist will develop as you become increasingly aware of the subtlety of the lies you believe. Cultural lies can be difficult to see because you've grown up them. Generational lies can be challenging because no one in the family may be willing to talk about them. Demonic lies can be the most subtle as the enemy is a master at what he does.

DISCIPLESHIP AND THE PRAYERS OF OTHERS

There are going to be many times when your ability to resist will come from the prayers of other brothers and sisters in Christ. "But encourage one another day after day, as long as it is still called Today, so that none of you will be hardened by the deceitfulness of sin" (Hebrews 4:13). Do not miss the blessing and relief that comes from asking brothers and sisters to stand and pray for you!

Your ability to resist will also increase as you grow in the Scriptures. Knowing God's Word will allow you to identify lies more easily and quickly. Biblical knowledge will also arm you with specific truth with which you can slice through lies. When wielded correctly, the Word of God contains great power. Paul calls the Scriptures the "sword of the Spirit" in Ephesians 6:17. As you learn to rightly handle the sword, your ability to identify specific lies and reject them with specific truth will increase.

By exercising the discipline of resistance, we stand firm in our faith, coming against initial lies and dealing with them immediately. In this way, these lies are not given room to do further damage. No matter the source of the attack in our lives, when we turn into the lie with the truth of Jesus in the power of the Spirit, the lie will fall off of us without damaging us. We cannot live faithfully to the Lord in the Way of Rest without becoming skilled in resisting temptation.

RESPONDING

This is what we have been working toward. Responding is simply obeying what God has given you to do. Responding is the posture of a person ready to go as God leads. After receiving direction from the Lord and resisting sin, the world, and Satan, you will respond faithfully to God's word. This gets you where God wants you: trusting Him to lead you. Everything we've built in the Way of Rest leads to obedience. This is where your belief is proved. It's easy to say, "I believe." It's much harder to follow.

We can have so many different attitudes toward obedience. It's weakness, or obligation. It's overbearing. It stifles uniqueness. It's not fun or pleasurable. However, Jesus says that obedience is the natural product of love. "If you love Me, you will keep My commandments" (John 14:15). The one who loves Jesus loves doing what Jesus says to do. By obeying the Lord you will get to see the wonders of the Lord. The only reason Israel got to experience God's power in parting the Red Sea is because they followed God. The only reason Joshua saw the walls of Jericho fall, or David slew Goliath, or Peter walked on water, or Paul was delivered from his spiritual blindness is because they all followed where God led them. Obedience will lead you to treasure chests of God's power and life. It should be no surprise to you that the enemy attacks attitudes toward obedience.

In addition to being a product of love, obedience is a mark of being a disciple. In His Great Commission, Jesus charges His disciples by saying, "Go therefore and make disciples of all the nations, baptizing them in the name of the Father and the Son and the Holy Spirit, *teaching them to observe all that I commanded you*; and lo, I am with you always, even to the end of the age" (Matthew 28:19–20, emphasis added).

Hebrews 11 lists seventeen individuals who followed God's direction in their lives, like Noah, Abraham, and Moses. These men and women have incredible life stories that go in many different directions, with some even ending in death. The commonality in all of them is that they followed where God led. While their obedience was not perfect and they wrestled with God's faithfulness, they stayed the course.

Take notice of the five disciplines in each of their lives:

1. They reflected on the faithfulness of God.
2. They released their anxiety or issues.
3. They received direction from the Lord.
4. They resisted sin, the world, and Satan.
5. They responded faithfully.

This is the recipe of the Way of Rest at work.

Building on the examples of Hebrews 11, Hebrews 12:1–2 exhorts us to run God's race without allowing anything to hinder our faithfulness:

> Therefore, since we have so great a cloud of witnesses surrounding us, let us also lay aside every encumbrance and the sin which so easily entangles us, and let us run with endurance the race that is set before us, fixing our eyes on Jesus, the author and perfecter of faith, who for the joy set before Him endured the cross, despising the shame, and has sat down at the right hand of the throne of God.

We are called to throw away everything that keeps us from running the race God has for us. This is the discipline of responding. This is the discipline of living continuously faithful to the leading of God for our lives.

RESPONDING TECHNIQUES

ALL THINGS

You do not pick and choose the parts of God's Word you like and only obey those. To walk with God is to believe Him in *all* things. Therefore, you follow God in your finances, marriage, sexuality, parenting, dieting, exercise, citizenship, prioritizing, and everything else He leads you in.[18]

God gives us three types of commands: relational, directional, and moral.

1. **Relational Response**: Be faithful to the Lord by obeying in the relationships He has for you. As He leads you to have a proper relationship with Him, be faithful. As He leads you to have a proper relationship in marriage, be faithful. As He leads you to be faithful in business, ministry, or family relationships, be faithful.

2. **Directional Response**: Be faithful to the Lord by going in the directions He leads you. God will lead you to places and people. Go. God led Israel to the Promised Land. He led Jesus to Galilee. He led Philip to an Ethiopian eunuch. He led Paul to Rome. Be sensitive to who or where God leads you. Whoever or wherever He is leading you is where He is.

3. **Moral Response**: Be faithful to your Father by dealing with the moral issues He wants to deal with in you. In 1 Peter 1:15, God says, "Be holy as I am holy." When you receive words from God dealing with moral issues, resist the temptation to ignore them and respond.

DISCIPLESHIP/COMMUNITY

Isn't it always easier to diet or exercise when everyone you know is dieting and exercising? Faithfully responding to God's words can be much easier when you're surrounded by others who are also obedient. You will have people around you to encourage you, sympathize with you, and hold you accountable.

Oftentimes people will reduce obedience to morality. Following God becomes about what you do not do and is no longer about having intimacy with Him and going where He leads. Get this: not a single life recorded in Hebrews 11 is there because of their morality. Every great person of faith is listed because they went where God led them and did what God asked them to do. Be careful that your obedience is not limited to morality. Go where God has for you to go and do what God has for you to do.

It won't be unusual for God's direction for your life to seem "crazy." Isaiah 55:8–9 says,

> "For My thoughts are not your thoughts,
> Nor are your ways My ways," declares the Lord.
> "For as the heavens are higher than the earth,
> So are My ways higher than your ways
> And My thoughts than your thoughts."

Do not be surprised when God's ways are not your ways. One way of knowing that you're in the will of God is disbelief about where you are. "There's no way I could have ever gotten here by myself!" Or, you cannot believe you are who you are. "I know me. There's no way I could be the person I am today by myself!" You cannot believe you get to talk with God. "I'm in relationship with the Father, Son, and Holy Spirit!" Ah! Faithfulness! The treasures of obedience are multiplied! Now God gets the glory and all you want is more.

THE GREAT TRAINING SUMMARY: 1 PETER 5:6–11

I want you to see all five disciplines together in one place. 1 Peter 5:6–11 is one of the great training summaries in all the Bible. I've inserted the names of the five disciplines in the Way of Rest so you can see these all together.

> Therefore, humble yourselves under the mighty hand of God, that He may exalt you at the proper time (***reflecting***), casting all your anxiety on Him, because He cares for you (***releasing, receiving***). Be of sober spirit, be on the alert, your adversary, the devil, prowls around like a roaring lion, seeking someone to devour. But resist him, firm in your faith, knowing that the same experiences of suffering are being accomplished by your brethren who are in the world (***resisting***). After you have suffered for a little while the God of all grace, who called you to His eternal glory in Christ, will Himself perfect, confirm, strengthen, and establish you. To Him be dominion forever and ever. Amen (***responding***)."

The five disciplines of the Way of Rest are reflection, releasing, receiving, resisting, and responding. Reflection is the foundation of the rest. We are always consciously aware of our love relationship with the Father, Son, and Holy Spirit. Every discipline has specific techniques that can be learned.

There are other techniques in each category that we did not cover. Fasting, for example, is a very powerful technique in the Lord. However, detailing all the available techniques in Scripture is beyond the scope of this book.[19] As you develop these practices in your faith, you will experience more of God's presence and promises in your life. None of these will keep you from the war, but they will equip you in how to deal with it as Jesus did.

CONCLUSION

Now, instead of Jesus on the boat in the middle of the Sea of Galilee, it's you. You're not on the Sea with the disciples. Rather, you're with family or co-workers. You all receive threatening news that seems catastrophic. Everyone else is running scared, as the fear of the unknown and the panic of being out-of-control begins to choke them. One at a time they notice that you're not responding like they are.

"Don't you care?" One demands. "What's wrong with you?" another blasts.

While those around you fall apart, you walk through the same storm at rest in the love and faithfulness of the Almighty God. Full of the Holy Spirit, in the name of Jesus, and according to the will of the Father, you speak peace and life into a "death" situation. They see it. Their angry questions change to interested questions: "How do you stay calm?" "What's different about you?" Doors open for the Gospel that have been shut for a long time.

This is the Way of Rest. This is Jesus' Kingdom recipe for living in the promises of God. This is what it looks like to be a disciple. Paul writes in Philippians 4:9, "The things you have learned and received and heard and seen in me, practice these things, and the God of peace will be with you." And he says in Philippians 3:17, "Brethren, join in following my example, and observe those who walk according to the same pattern (recipe) you have in us."

May you enjoy intimacy with your Father, Jesus, and the Holy Spirit. May you be filled with grace, mercy, love, and strength. May you take on the yoke of Jesus and continue to learn from Him. May you excel as a warrior. And as you walk in the fullness of Jesus, may you go with passion to train others as you have been trained.

"The grace of the Lord Jesus Christ, and the love of God, and the fellowship of the Holy Spirit, be with you all." — 2 Corinthians 13:14

TRAINING: CHAPTER WORK

Start this work by reflecting on the role your Father has for you in relationship with Him. He is always initiating, you are always responding. Bless Him for His initiating love for you. Thank Him for all the clarity He's bringing you. Allow yourself to hear encouraging words from Him for your faithfulness to get to this point. Write anything that you think and/or feel here.

To finish, you're going to walk through each of the disciplines to get practice in each.

1. Spend time reflecting on God's wisdom for your life. Soak in Him and the glory of His divine leading in every area of life.

2. Identify the areas of your life that are causing you anxiety. Release each one specifically to the Lord, declaring His faithfulness over each one.

3. Ask the Lord to give you clear direction in an area of your life where you have need.

4. Begin to resist whatever hesitation you may be having. Take every word, feeling, or image captive that may be coming up that threatens your obedience.

5. Go! Faithfully follow whatever God has given you.

That is the Way of Rest in action. Continue to work the Eph 1. Observe all five ingredients in the diagram. Walk in the presence and promises of the Father, Son, and Holy Spirit.

BE

THE WAY OF REST

NOTES

CHAPTER 4

1. Three times in Isaiah the prophet gives words about the relationship between the coming Messiah and the Holy Spirit. In Isaiah 11:1–5, 42:1–4, and 61:1–3, Isaiah prophecies that the coming Messiah will be full of the Spirit. His wisdom, character, power, and mission will all be works of the Spirit in Him. The role of the Spirit in the Messiah's life was not to be secondary or minimal. Rather, the Spirit is responsible for the life and ministry of the Messiah.

2. Notice in this passage that the application of Jesus' work in our lives is the role of the Holy Spirit. Many people who quote this verse still suffer condemnation. Many suffer because they have an unhealthy relationship with the Holy Spirit. This is living in Trinitarian imbalance.

3. In addition to Jesus' teachings, the rest of Scripture testifies to the reality of one God. Exodus 20:1–7, Isaiah 45:5–6, and James 2:19 are some examples of the Scriptures teaching one God.

4. This is not intended to be an exhaustive study of Jesus' teachings on the Trinity. For a fuller discussion, read Bruce Ware's Father, Son, and Holy Spirit: Relationships, Roles, and Relevance.

5. The Holy Spirit is often called the Spirit of God or the Spirit of Christ. He is called this as a demonstration of the intimacy that exists between the persons of the Trinity. Similarly, Jesus can say, "If you had known Me, you would have known My Father also" (John 14:7). This is possible because of the degree of intimacy that exists among the Father, Son, and Holy Spirit.

6. See also Titus 3:3–7 for another excellent example.

CHAPTER 5

7. We see these listed right next to each other in Ephesians 2:1–2: "And you were dead in your trespasses and sins, in which you formerly walked according to the course of this world, according to the prince of the power of the air, of the spirit that is now working in the sons of disobedience."

8. To be sure, when I say Satan, I mean more than the angel formerly called Lucifer. Satan himself is not personally doing all of these things. He has an army that orderly, systematically, and deliberately carries out his works. Again, Paul writes in Ephesians 6:12, "For our struggle is not against flesh and blood, but against the rulers, against the powers, against the world forces of this darkness, against the spiritual forces of wickedness in the heavenly places." Satan's effectiveness happens through the combined forces of his spiritual army.

9. I have found Karl Payne's book *Spiritual Warfare* to be the best and most sober book available on the topic.

10. For more examples see Matthew 16:21–23, Ephesians 4:26–27, and 1 Peter 5:6–11.

11. The NIV translates Paul's flesh as the "sinful nature." The Apostle John uses light/dark imagery to convey the same message. Darkness can be from Satan, the world, or a reference to the flesh/sinful nature of man.

12. Other lists of sins are given in Galatians 5:19–21 and other Scriptures.

CHAPTER 7

13. Freedom is a deep topic too expansive to cover here in great detail. I have written another book, Fortified: From Fear, Anxiety, and Bondage to Freedom and Power in Jesus, that covers this extensively.

14. For another example of deliverance in the Psalms, see Psalm 107, a psalm of deliverance for four different types of people: wanderers, those dwelling in darkness, the rebellious, and unethical businessmen.

15. In Joel 2, God promised there would be a day when He would send His Spirit on His people in a way He had never come before. The coming of the Spirit at Pentecost was another fulfillment of a promise of God made long ago.

16. Jesus teaches in John 3 that whoever gives their lives to Him is born again by the Holy Spirit.

CHAPTER 8

17. Graham Cooke has a three volume set called The Way of the Warrior that is a great read on living life as a warrior in the Kingdom.

18. It's unfortunate that very few pastors and church leaders address God's teaching on diet and exercise. You will quickly discover the connection between your spiritual vitality and your physical condition. You cannot have a terrible diet and be inactive and expect that you will walk in the blessings of God. While Jesus never laid out a specific diet plan, He did eat in a way that produced a healthy body. I am not a dietician, but the book What Would Jesus Eat?

is a good place to start to understand God's word on dieting. Furthermore, while Jesus never said anything about exercising, it's estimated he walked over 3,000 miles during His ministry. Being physically active and eating healthily are steps of obedience the Spirit will lead you to.

19. Richard Foster's *Celebration of Discipline* is the best text on many of the techniques of our faith.

Made in the USA
San Bernardino, CA
30 November 2016